Business Allstars

The Adventures of
Nobel Merchant & Hannah Watson

By
Gaylen K. Bunker, MBA, CPA

D1377515

BusinessAllStars, Salt Lake City, Utah 84109
Copyright 2014 © by Gaylen K. Bunker
All rights reserved
Printed in the United States of America

The cover photo is of the Eiffel Tower in Paris
It was taken by Gaylen K. Bunker

www.businessallstars.com is a support web site
where calculation and assessment tools may be found.

Table of Contents

Acknowledgements

I want to express appreciation for the generous contributions made by my wife, Diane, who has read and reread the manuscript many times and given extremely valuable input. I also want to thank her for helping me to realize the importance of accounting as a fundamental tool in everyone's tool bag. I also want to express appreciation for the many students I have had the privilege of teaching these many twenty-five years and all they have taught me.

Gaylen K. Bunker

FRAMED

Learning Objectives

An understanding of:
Spreadsheets
The Accounting Equation
Assets, Liabilities and Equity
Double Entry Accounting System
Balance Sheet
Income Statement
Statement of Retained Earnings
Statement of Cash Flows (Direct)
Statement of Cash Flows (Indirect)
Operating Activity
Investing Activity
Financing Activity

Spreadsheet Tools found at
www.businessallstars.com/calculator

Assessment found at
www.businessallstars.com/assessment

Saturday Morning

Nobel Merchant put away his breakfast dishes and thought to himself of all the possibilities this beautiful Spring Saturday morning offered. He looked out the window above the sink at the thermometer hanging from a decorative post just outside. It read seventy-two degrees. His fingers began to itch at the possibilities waiting for him out on the road. That new bike he had just purchased had only been out a couple of times and today was perfect for another long ride.

Nobel gazed up at the blue sky and then down toward the garden beneath him. As he panned across the scene, he suddenly caught sight of the new neighbor that had moved in next door. She was on her deck holding a watering can, lightly sprinkling a large flower pot. He thought to himself how lovely she looked.

His thoughts began to drift back to the workshop where he kept his bike when he realized she had noticed him at the window and was waving to him. A little embarrassed that he was caught watching her, he sheepishly waved back.

With her free hand she gestured for him to come outside. She stepped back, set the watering can down and motioning to the gate that separated the two yards began to walk toward it.

"Well, I suppose I need to be neighborly," he thought to himself and worked his way toward the back door.

The two yards were separated by a six foot fence that generally provided excellent privacy. When the fence was originally built, the two neighbors, who owned the homes at that time, had decided to place a quaint white arbor that broke the fence near the rear of each home. A white picket gate with a half-circle top complimented the arch of the arbor.

When he exited his home, he turned to see her standing at the gate. As she approached he couldn't help but notice how stunningly beautiful she looked framed by the arbor. He guessed that she was probably about thirty, but if she was indeed that old she could easily have passed for someone much younger.

"I'm your new neighbor. My name is Hannah Watson and I moved in about a month ago, but this is the first chance I've had to make contact with you."

"It's good to meet you. I wasn't sure who moved in after the Razelburgers left."

"It's just me, but I'm in desperate need of your help."

Instantly, his thoughts jumped to plumbing or another kind of fixit job that a handyman might help with. He liked to putter, but never represented himself as someone with the knowledge to impose his abilities on others?"

"Some of the other neighbors told me that you are a financial wizard, consult with companies and put on seminars teaching basic accounting and financial statements."

"I'm not sure wizard is the term I would use. I do consult on a whole host of business topics, but lately my teaching and business seminars have kept me pretty busy."

"I really hate to impose, but I'm in real trouble. My father passed away several months ago and left a part interest in a small company to me. I'm his only child and my career has been modeling. I know that physical beauty is a temporary gift so I have tried to get involved with the business and understand what is going on." She stopped and looked at him with all earnestness. "Do you have a minute we could talk?"

He turned and motioned to a white round picnic table in the shade of a large maple tree in his backyard. "Why don't we sit and you can tell me more." He led her to the table and took a seat, all the time thinking the contrast between them was stark. He was in his Saturday sweats ready to dive into some physical activity and she looked like she just walked out of the pages of a fashion magazine.

She continued her story: "I began to think there were some strange things happening with the company. Things just didn't seem right. The heads of sales, production and accounting were all very nice to me, but seemed guarded. Then just last week I got a call to meet my father's partner, Victor Timothy in his office at ten o'clock at night. I thought it rather odd, but went to the appointment anyway."

"When I got there I found Victor lying on the floor. He had been shot in the chest and barely alive. He motioned toward the bookcase and stammered: 'The shoebox, the shoebox.' Then he died in my arms. I looked around for the shoebox and saw a gun lying on the floor behind the door. I don't know what possessed me, maybe it was some stupid idea the police wouldn't see it there and so I went and picked it up. Just as I did the police came into the room. I've been accused of the murder and am only out on bail awaiting the arraignment."

"Someone set me up and framed me for this murder. I have a wonderful attorney, her name is Mary Payson, and she was able to get hold of the shoe box but neither the police nor her see anything in it. It's just a bunch of financial records. Do you think you could look at them for me?"

4

"Well, probably so," he responded.

With that she was up and jogging toward the gate and her home. He was captured and all thoughts of a bike ride flew out of his mind. He watched her all the way to her back door and back again holding a small red shoebox. On top of the box she balanced a laptop computer.

"I thought we could use a computer, if that's okay?" she said as she approached the table.

"Oh, sure, that would be great." He took the shoebox, sat it on the table, opened it, and began looking through the papers as she set up the computer.

"I really appreciate you taking the time to do this. I have been in a panic since this whole thing started." Her flawless composure belied the turmoil she suggested that raged inside of her.

"I think we're going to have to reconstruct some accounting detail to make any sense of all this," he said as he examined the papers. "Do you know much about spreadsheets?"

"Not really. I'm starting from ground zero," she confessed.

He leaned close to her to see the screen and guided the arrow to the bottom left-hand corner of the screen where he clicked on the 'Start' button. A menu opened on the side. Finding a reference to a spreadsheet program, he clicked and waited for it to appear. "A spreadsheet is a grid of rows and columns where we can enter words, amounts, formulas, or references. It will help us organize the data."

"I think I've seen this before," she admitted.

"That's great. I'm going to create a format to work from."

Figure 1-1
(Left side of equal sign)

				Assets			
	Cash	A/R	Inv.	Sup.	F/A	A/D	=
1							
2							
3							
4							
5							
6							
7							
8							
9							
10							
11							
12							
13							
14							

When he finished entering the layout he turned to her. "I'm going to use some abbreviations for the economy of space. Let me define what I've created here."

"A/R represents Accounts Receivable; Inv. for Inventory; Sup. for Supplies; F/A for Fixed Assets; A/D for Accumulated Depreciation; A/P for Accounts Payable; N/P for Notes Payable; LTD for Long-term debt; C/S for Common Stock; and R/E for Retained Earnings."

"I have two groups of accounts. Those on the left side are Assets and those on the right are Claims. Do you know what I mean by those two categories?"

6

Figure 1-1 (continued)
(Right side of equal sign)

Claims (Liabilities & Equity)					
A/P	N/P	LTD	C/S	R/E	Desc.
					Beg Bal

She thought for a moment. "Assets are things of value the company owns and uses to make the business operate."

"Excellent definition, do you know what Claims are?"

"Not really," she responded.

"Everything on the right side of the equal sign show who has a Claim on the Assets of the business. Even though the business is an entity separate from the owners or suppliers, the providers of financing have a Claim on the business until the obligation is settled. The equal sign is extremely important. It is the one thing that

7

is absolute in accounting. The Assets must equal the Claims."

"This is called the double entry system and means that every time the business enters into a transaction, such as the payment of cash, they must record at least two entries into this grid, so that the Assets will always equal the Claims."

"When the Assets go up, the Claims must go up and when the Assets go down the Claims must go down by an equal amount. Sometimes one Asset will go up and another Asset will go down or a Claim will go and another Claim will go down. The bottom line is that the Assets must always equal the Claims."

"I think I understand," she noted.

Account for Anything

He thought to himself that only ten minutes ago he had no idea she even existed and now they were deep into an exchange of ideas. It seemed so natural to be with her, as if he had known her for a long time. He was sure it was her open and friendly manner.

"The Assets are pretty straight forward and easy to understand: Cash, Inventory, Supplies, Fixed Assets. These are all tangible items."

"I've heard those terms, but how can you tell the difference between Inventory, Supplies, and Fixed Assets?"

"Let me see if I can make some sense of it. Inventories are items that are sold to customers. Supplies are relatively low-cost tangible items consumed by the company within a one year time frame. Fixed Assets are tangible items that are typically of high dollar value and will be used over many years."

"Think of the photo studio where you pose for a series of pictures. Many of the props, cameras, lights, and other equipment are Fixed Assets. What you are trying to generate are products to sell, the photos which are the Inventory. The incidental items, such as pins, tissues, and other disposable tangible things are Supplies. Does that help?"

"So things customers purchase, like the photos are the Inventory, incidental little things are the Supplies and expensive equipment are the Fixed Assets."

"You got it. There are two other accounts I've shown as Assets: A/R for Accounts Receivable and A/D for Accumulated Depreciation. When we talk about cash we can see the coins and paper money that represents an IOU from the federal government. Accounts Receivable is like a stack of paper IOUs from customers. They have

9

value, and in fact can be sold to a bank or collection agency for money."

"Accumulated Depreciation is what we call a contra-Asset. This means it is a negative Asset. It shows how much the Fixed Assets have been consumed, worn-out or used-up over the life of the Asset. If you purchase a camera for five thousand dollars you would record that in the Fixed Assets account. The camera may only last five years and then be worn out. Each year you use the camera you consume part of its value and so we record that consumption in the Accumulated Depreciation account. When we subtract the Accumulated Depreciation amount from the Fixed Asset balance at any point in time, we find what we call the Net Value of the Fixed Asset."

"I think I've got a handle on the Assets, but what about the Claims?" she asked.

"Let's take them one at a time. A/P or Accounts Payable are the result of the business purchasing Inventory and/or Supplies from vendors. If the vendors do not demand immediate payment and extend credit to the business, then an Account Payable is created. It is an Account Receivable on the vendor's books and they have a Claim on the purchaser's Assets as long as their account goes unpaid."

"What kinds of Accounts Payable would a photo studio have?" she asked.

"I suppose the studio would purchase photo print paper and various Supplies from a vendor. If they didn't pay with cash then the vendor would send an invoice requesting payment after a certain period of time. During the time between the acquisition of the Supplies and the actual payment of the invoice the balance due would appear on the studio's books as an Account Payable."

"This next one is N/P. Is that another payable?" she asked.

"That's right. It stands for Notes Payable. Sometimes a business like a photo studio will run out of cash. Maybe their customers haven't paid for their purchases yet, but they need to pay their suppliers. Maybe they need to pay salaries to the photographers and models, but haven't sold the finished photos yet. So they go to the bank and agree to get a short-term loan to carry them over for a few months. They sign a note and show it on their books as a Note Payable to the bank."

"The next account is LTD or Long-term Debt. This is a Claim by people who have lent money to the business. Sometimes those people are banks, but they may also be individuals. Whenever the business takes out a loan, they agree to repay the amount at a specified period of time, plus interest for the use of the money."

"What is the difference between Notes Payable and Long-Term Debts?"

"Mostly, it is how long it will take to pay off the obligation. Notes Payable will usually be repaid within the next twelve months. Long-Term Debts will usually be carried on a company's books for several years."

"What are these last two: C/S and R/E?"

"C/S is for Common Stock and R/E is for Retained Earnings. When someone purchases an ownership position in a business they can be issued stock certificates that represent their share or an equity Claim. They give money to the business to use in return for a promise to receive all the Earnings of the business."

"So my father and Victor were owners of the business. I know I inherited a 50% ownership in the business."

"Your Claim on the business would be shown on the books under this heading along with the other

11

Common Stock owners. If the owners decide not to take the Earnings out of the business each year, but instead leave them with the company to reinvest for growth, then we call this Retained Earnings. This account is like an Accounts Payable to the Owners and increases their Claim. So the combination of Common Stock and Retained Earnings shows the owner's total Claim on the Assets of the business."

"Are these all of the accounts? What I mean is, why did you list these particular ones and are there others that should be considered?"

"There are many other accounts we could enter into the grid, many on the Asset side and many on the Claims side. I've been looking at the year-end balance sheet that was in the shoebox and it appears to me that these accounts will accommodate most of the transactions that we will need to make."

"Okay," she said.

Figure 1-2
(Left side of equal sign)

	Assets						
	Cash	A/R	Inv.	Sup.	F/A	A/D	=
0	1000	500	200	100	6000	-1600	
1							

Hunting for Clues

He entered numbers into the grid (Figure 1-2) from a printed sheet he had taken from the shoebox.

"These are the amounts for the end of the prior period that we will enter into our grid on the first row as the beginning balances for this new period of transactions. The source document that I used was titled 'Balance Sheet for the year ending Apr 30'."

"I've seen that before. Victor, the man I'm accused of killing, showed it to me about the middle of May," she offered.

"There are several other loose papers in the box. I'm going to examine them one at a time and then try and make entries to the grid for each transaction," he instructed.

"That's fine. I'll try and pay attention. I suppose we are looking for any type of clue that could help lead to who the real murderer is?"

Figure 1-2 (continued)
(Right side of equal sign)

Claims (Liabilities & Equity)					
A/P	N/P	LTD	C/S	R/E	Desc.
300	100	1500	4000	300	Beg Bal

"That's right. Here is a deposit slip that shows a $3,000 deposit in the bank. There is a note on the slip that states it is from the sale of stock. Were you aware of any additional stock issued during May?"

"No, that is a complete surprise to me."

"It could be a clue, but then again maybe not. We will enter it into the grid as an addition of $3,000 to cash and increase to the owner's Claims in C/S or Common Stock (Figure 1-3)."

Figure 1-3
(Left side of equal sign)

	Assets						=
	Cash	A/R	Inv.	Sup.	F/A	A/D	
0	1000	500	200	100	6000	-1600	
1	3000						
2							

"This is that double entry thing, right?"

"That is exactly what we are doing. The Assets went up by $3,000 in cash and the Claims increased by the same amount in equity."

"If you didn't give that money for stock then either Victor did or stock was sold to someone other than you two. You had no knowledge of this transaction?" he queried.

"None whatsoever," she confessed.

Figure 1-4
(Left side of equal sign)

	Assets						=
	Cash	A/R	Inv.	Sup.	F/A	A/D	
0	1000	500	200	100	6000	-1600	
1	3000						
2			4000				
3							

14

"Let's continue, maybe there will be more. This next transaction is a purchase order for $4,000 of Inventory sent to Anderson Wholesale Distributors.

Figure 1-3 (continued)
(Right side of equal sign)

Claims (Liabilities & Equity)					
A/P	N/P	LTD	C/S	R/E	Desc.
300	100	1500	4000	300	Beg Bal
			3000		

There is a delivery slip for the same amount stapled to the back. You ordered Inventory for resale and received it."

"I see terms on the delivery notification of 2/10, net 30. That means that if you pay in ten days you can deduct 2% as a discount, but if not then you will pay the full amount in 30 days. So I assume you did not pay cash on delivery for the Inventory."

"I think that is our policy to pay some time later."

Figure 1-4 (continued)
(Right side of equal sign)

Claims (Liabilities & Equity)					
A/P	N/P	LTD	C/S	R/E	Desc.
300	100	1500	4000	300	Beg Bal
			3000		
4000					

"I can't see anything unusual here. It seems like a pretty standard and routine transaction."

"I would agree," she offered.

"To record this on the grid, I will add $4,000 to the Inv. or Inventory account and add the same amount, $4,000, to the "A/P" or Accounts Payable account for money we owe. With an entry on both sides of the equal sign we are still in balance, where the sum of all Assets is the same as the sum of all the Claims (Figure 1-4)."

"I think I'm beginning to understand. In a way it is a system," she recognized.

"It is a self-checking system. At least we know we are still in balance; we are never sure that we put everything in the correct account though."

"So there is still room for error?"

"That's right."

"This next slip of paper is interesting. It is a purchase order from a customer, Xtron, Inc. for $6,000 worth of products."

Figure 1-5
(Left side of equal sign)

	Assets						
	Cash	A/R	Inv.	Sup.	F/A	A/D	=
0	1000	500	200	100	6000	-1600	
1	3000						
2			4000				
3		6000					
4			-3000				
5							

"Why do you say it is interesting?"

16

"Usually there are notations that are placed on the P/O when it is received. This has nothing. Let's go ahead and record this item on the grid. There is no evidence to suggest the customer paid in advance or along with the P/O, so I will record this as an increase in A/R or Accounts Receivable for $6,000 and a corresponding increase in a Claim. Do you have any idea which Claim would be affected?"

"Oh dear, since we are going to get money, I don't think it is a payable or debt, so it must be "C/S" or Common Stock. But in a way, that doesn't seem right."

"I'm going to record it as Revenue. When we sell products it is like we are getting a big bucket of Earnings that belong to the stock holders. So I will record it under the heading R/E or Retained Earnings (Figure `1-5)."

"Really?" she questioned.

"That's right." He shuffled through the papers in the box. "Oh here is the rest of the story. It is a corresponding delivery record for $3,000 that shows the

Figure 1-5 (continued)
(Right side of equal sign)

Claims (Liabilities & Equity)					
A/P	N/P	LTD	C/S	R/E	Desc.
300	100	1500	4000	300	Beg Bal
			3000		
4000					
				6000	Revenue
				-3000	C.O.G.S.

inventory going to Xtron and there is a reference to the P/O number. I'm going to record this as a negative $3,000 going out of Inv. or Inventory and a negative

$3,000 Cost of Goods Sold in "R/E" or Retained
Earnings. So Retained Earnings shows Revenue from the
sale and the Cost of Goods Sold going out of the
business. The net effect is $3,000 of Earnings or Gross
Profit in Retained Earnings (Figure 1-5)."

"What did you say Retained Earnings are?"

"They are a payable to the owners for Earnings
that were generated but not yet paid. In this case we have
Inventory that costs $3,000 that is subtracted from the
Revenue of $6,000. So the Inventory cost the company
$3,000 and then was marked up and sold to generate a
$3,000 profit. All gross profits belong to the owners."

"Do you see anything strange that would give us a
clue or shed some light on who really killed my co-
owner?"

Figure 1-6
(Left side of equal sign)

	Assets						=
	Cash	A/R	Inv.	Sup.	F/A	A/D	
0	1000	500	200	100	6000	-1600	
1	3000						
2			4000				
3		6000					
4			-3000				
5	-2000				2000		
6							

"Not exactly," He said as he rummaged through
the box extracting another slip of paper. "Here is a
canceled check for the purchase of equipment. It is for
$2,000 to Jabberwocky Equipment and Leasing

Company. Do you remember any new equipment being acquired by the company?"

"We installed a new computer in the accounting department."

"That would do it. Where do you think I should put this on the grid?"

"I don't think it is Inventory because we are not going to sell it to a customer. It is going to last for several years and so it probably should go into the "F/A" or fixed Asset account."

"Good," he encouraged.

"I don't see where it would go on the Claims side though."

"We paid cash and so it is a decrease in Cash of $2,000 (Figure 1-6).

Figure 1-6 (continued)
(Right side of equal sign)

Claims (Liabilities & Equity)					
A/P	N/P	LTD	C/S	R/E	Desc.
300	100	1500	4000	300	Beg Bal
			3000		
4000					
				6000	Revenue
				-3000	C.O.G.S.

"Wait a minute, I thought you said we had to balance and these are both on the Asset side."

19

"One is an Asset addition and one is an Asset reduction and so we are still in balance."

"Interesting, so we don't always need to affect both sides of the equal sign," she mused.

He nodded as he pulled another paper from the shoebox: "This next document is a deposit in the bank for $5,500 received from Xtron. Evidently, they paid on some of the bills they owed. Where do you think we should enter this?"

Figure 1-7

(Left side of equal sign)

	Assets						
	Cash	A/R	Inv.	Sup.	F/A	A/D	=
0	1000	500	200	100	6000	-1600	
1	3000						
2			4000				
3		6000					
4			-3000				
5	-2000				2000		
6	5500	-5500					
7	-2000						
8							

"You keep asking me that. Is this turning into an accounting seminar with a quiz after each transaction?"

"I'm just trying to make sure you understand what we are doing," he responded.

"Okay, we got the cash and so I would add $5,500 to Cash and reduce "A/R" or Accounts Receivable, offsetting one Asset with another," she said with pride (Figure 1-7).

"Very good," He said pulling another slip from the box. "Here is a payroll note. It says that $2,000 was due for salaries and attached is a bank document recognizing the payment. Does this sound reasonable?"

"I think that's pretty routine---I would say it is okay," she responded.

"This is an operating cost or expense. It is a necessary part of doing business and shows value going

Figure 1-7 (continued)
(Right side of equal sign)

Claims (Liabilities & Equity)					
A/P	N/P	LTD	C/S	R/E	Desc.
300	100	1500	4000	300	Beg Bal
			3000		
4000					
				6000	Revenue
				-3000	C.O.G.S.
				-2000	Opr. Exp.

out of the company. When value is lost then it is an expense."

"I know cash will be reduced because it was paid out, but I'm not sure where to record an expense."

"It further reduces the Earnings of the company and so it will be a reduction in the "R/E" or Retained Earnings."

21

"That's curious."

"Curious, in what way?" he asked.

"All these entries are raising a lot of questions in my mind, but I'm not sure I'm getting any better information about who is the murderer. Is there anything here that you are seeing that stands out?" she asked.

"Can we hold that question until we get to the end?"

"Certainly," she confirmed.

Pulling out another slip of paper he read, "Memo: $500 of depreciation on equipment for the period." He looked at her. "It looks like your equipment is slowly wearing out."

Figure 1-8
(Left side of equal sign)

		Assets					
	Cash	A/R	Inv.	Sup.	F/A	A/D	=
0	1000	500	200	100	6000	-1600	
1	3000						
2			4000				
3		6000					
4			-3000				
5	-2000				2000		
6	5500	-5500					
7	-2000						
8						-500	
9							

"I know we had to get a new computer because the old one was totally obsolete. I wouldn't have any idea where to put this...wait a minute---you said we record it in "A/D" or Accumulated Depreciation. So I guess it would be a negative $500 there."

"Score a victory for you," he said with pride.

She seemed to beam with the first big smile of the day. Her absolute radiance and natural beauty made him wonder how anyone could think to try and destroy such a masterpiece. Then he caught himself, could it be jealousy he wondered. "This is a reduction of value from the business and so it is an expense (Figure 1-8)."

"You mean the other side of the entry is to "R/E" as we are further reducing Earnings?"

"You've got it," he congratulated.

Figure 1-8 (continued)
(Right side of equal sign)

Claims (Liabilities & Equity)					
A/P	N/P	LTD	C/S	R/E	Desc.
300	100	1500	4000	300	Beg Bal
			3000		
4000					
				6000	Revenue
				-3000	C.O.G.S.
				-2000	Opr. Exp.
				-500	Dep. Exp.

She beamed again with great satisfaction. "You are either a great teacher or I'm a pretty quick student. I'll accept the former."

"I'll agree with the later."

"What's next?" she asked.

"There aren't too many documents left, I hope we find something in the rest of this stuff," he said as he rummaged around in the box. "Here is a cancelled check to Anderson Wholesale Distributors for $3,600. Here is another check to the IRS for the payment of income taxes of $200 and a third check for $50 to Pembroke Office Supplies."

"It looks to me like they are all a reduction of cash and so would be entered as negatives in the Cash account," she offered.

Figure 1-9
(Left side of equal sign)

	Assets						
	Cash	A/R	Inv.	Sup.	F/A	A/D	=
0	1000	500	200	100	6000	-1600	=
1	3000						
2			4000				
3		6000					
4			-3000				
5	-2000				2000		
6	5500	-5500					
7	-2000						
8						-500	
9	-3600						
10	-200						
11	-50			50			
12							

"Excellent, do you have any idea where the offsetting entries would be?" he asked.

24

"Not really."

"The first one $3,600 is a payment on the purchases we made for Inventory when we promised to pay later. It would reduce our obligation and so would be a negative in the "A/P" or Accounts Payable (Figure 1-9). The next one is an Expense for income taxes."

"An Expense, so it would further reduce our Earnings and be a negative to "R/E" or Retained Earnings (Figure 1-9)," she jumped in.

Figure 1-9 (continued)
(Right side of equal sign)

Claims (Liabilities & Equity)					
A/P	N/P	LTD	C/S	R/E	Desc.
300	100	1500	4000	300	Beg Bal.
			3000		
4000					
				6000	Revenue
				-3000	C.O.G.S.
				-2000	Opr. Exp.
				-500	Dep. Exp.
-3600					
				-200	Inc. Tax

"Good, the third is a payment for the acquisition of office Supplies and so would increase the "Sup." or

25

Supplies Asset (Figure 1-9)," he said.

"Do we ever reduce the Supplies account? It can't just keep growing because I know we are constantly using them and so we keep buying them," she wondered.

"We expense them through an estimation of how much we think has been used or we actually count what we have left in the storeroom, subtract that from the total in the account and expense what has been used up."

Figure 1-10
(Left side of equal sign)

	Assets						
	Cash	A/R	Inv.	Sup.	F/A	A/D	=
0	1000	500	200	100	6000	-1600	=
1	3000						
2			4000				
3		6000					
4			-3000				
5	-2000				2000		
6	5500	-5500					
7	-2000						
8						-500	
9	-3600						
10	-200						
11	-50			50			
12	-70						
13	1580	1000	1200	150	8000	-2100	=
14							

"There is one last memo in the box," he said.
"What is it?" she wanted to know.

"It is the payment of dividends to stockholders for $70. I don't see a cancelled check so we may have to examine the bank statement."

"What does the memo say?"

"That's all, just payment of dividends to stockholders for $70. Did you receive a dividend?" he asked.

Figure 1-10 (continued)
(Right side of equal sign)

Claims (Liabilities & Equity)					
A/P	N/P	LTD	C/S	R/E	Desc.
300	100	1500	4000	300	Beg Bal.
			3000		
4000					
				6000	Revenue
				-3000	C.O.G.S.
				-2000	Opr. Exp.
				-500	Dep. Exp.
-3600					
				-200	Inc. Tax
				-70	Dividend
700	100	1500	7000	530	End. Bal.

"I did. I received $20 on the 2,000 shares I inherited from my father."

27

"This is interesting. Let's record this in the grid and then summarize each column. That will give us an ending balance for the period."

"Is that all we can do?"

"No this is just the first step. We are going to generate financial statements and see what they tell us."

"Really!" she exclaimed.

"We are going to take this thing to the point where it will give us every bit of information we need. For some strange reason I believe in your innocence and would like to help all that I can."

"Would it be okay, if you don't mind, I'll run home and get a little refreshment for us," she offered.

"Great," he agreed.

She got up, turned and walked toward the gate. He watched her and wondered to himself how the morning had turned out very differently than he had planned.

His final grid with ending balances reflected all the transactions from the shoebox (Figure 1-10).

Recap What We Know

He looked up to see her approaching the gate holding a tray. A pale blue oxford cloth, button down collar shirt hung open in front revealing that she had slipped it over the top of her sun dress. On the tray were a pitcher, two glasses and a plate of pastries. He jumped up and hurried to the gate, opened and held it as she passed through. He followed her to the table where she placed the tray.

The sun had moved in the sky, but the table was still in full shade. He checked his watch and it was almost ten.

"Oh how foolish of me. I'm taking your whole morning and only thinking of myself and my problems. I didn't even ask if you had other plans," she sheepishly offered.

"I was only going take a ride out to the point on my bike, but that can certainly wait."

"Sometimes I lose focus and have a tendency to only think of myself. Some say I'm self-centered and it is only natural because I'm a model. They assume I only think of how I look and what I want. That isn't true. For some reason people hold back and I sense a barrier. It really is a little difficult. I am conscious of my appearance; I have to because it is my job. I don't really think I'm any more self-absorbed than other people, but it is only natural for people to think that."

Her rambling caught him a little off-guard. He didn't quite know what to say and then blurted out, "I think everyone looks more inward than outward. I'm only too glad to help, because you are in a tough spot, I'm your new neighbor and I want us to be friends."

The last comment about being a friend seemed to really resonate with her. "Will you please be my friend?" she asked.

"There is no question about it," he assured.

With that comment she seemed to release some tension and relax a little more. He also realized that saying the word friend changed the way he looked at her. He sensed that every male is a potential predatory animal looking at every female as a possible conquest or challenge. He supposed that females see males in much the same way. He sensed the initial sexual tension between them, but now by saying the word, friend, it seemed to change the way they looked at each other. They were no longer sizing each other up, but together, as allies, were facing an external challenge.

"I don't know that I've had a lot of friends in my life," she offered. "What do you think it means to be a friend?"

"I've thought about this a great deal through the years and I think it means to sacrifice for the other person. Also, to ask questions with a sincere interest and listen to what they have to say, really trying to understand. Lastly, it means to encourage them toward their own success.

"Wow that is amazing. I've never heard it put so succinctly. That is really great. I'm going to try and do those things, beginning with you."

He smiled at her and then continued, "Why don't we recap what we know."

"I think we should. I know one thing for sure," she stated.

"What is that?"

"I know a lot more about accounting than I ever did before. I know Assets have to balance with Claims. I know Assets are the things of value that support Revenue

30

generating activities. I know Claims show all the parties who have a financial interest in the Assets of the company."

"Not only that, but if the company were to ever go out of business and the Assets had to be liquidated or converted to cash, the money generated would be given to everyone who has a Claim."

"I also know that just as Cash is an IOU from the government, an Account Receivable is an IOU from a customer, has value and can be traded or sold to someone else. I know the difference between Inventory, Supplies, and equipment or Fixed Assets. I know that as equipment wears out we record the loss in value in the Accumulated Depreciation account."

"The result of subtracting Accumulated Depreciation from Fixed Assets is what is called the net Fixed Assets. That is what it is worth today as opposed to what we paid for it," he added.

"I know that an Account Payable on our books is the same thing as an Account Receivable on the books of those who sell us things and we haven't paid yet. They are IOUs from us to them."

She continued. "I know that a Note Payable is a short-term obligation, like within one year, and Long-Term Debts are liabilities that span a much longer time, perhaps even several years."

"Liabilities, Claims, and Debts are all terms for financial obligations to those who have extended credit to us and have a Claim on our Assets until the commitment is paid," he pointed out.

"I know the owner's Claims on the Assets are represented in two accounts: Common Stock and Retained Earnings. The first is money they directly invested in the company and the second is a payable to them for Earnings that were reinvested in the company on their behalf and not yet paid."

She went on, "I also know that Revenues are the gross Earnings of the company and as value goes out of the business then we recognize cost and expenses that reduce those Earnings."

"I might warn you that I have made all this very simple with very few entries. If a company had thousands of transactions and entries, they would summarize all Revenues in an account and Expenses in various accounts. Then at the end of the period they would add up the Revenues, subtract all the Expenses and put the net difference into Retained Earnings. It is the responsibility of the owners to determine if they will leave all the Earnings in the company or pay some out in the form of dividends."

"So as an owner, I should be consulted as to if and when a dividend is paid?" she asked.

"That is exactly right. Not only that but you should be consulted about any new stock issued or any new owners added to the company," he instructed.

"I guess that brings us back to the issue of any clues regarding the murder. I was never involved in the sale of new stock or the payment of a dividend, but I should have been," she fumed.

"You're absolutely correct," he agreed.

She poured a tall glass from the pitcher. "I think whoever was involved in that is the one who set me up and framed me. It all makes sense now."

"I hope it is that simple, but we need to explore every possibility," he cautioned.

"What else could it be?"

"I'm not sure, but feel we need to go to the next step."

"What is that?"

"I'd like to construct some financial statements from the data," he explained.

Make a Statement

"I'm going to create four financial statement from the data that will help us identify areas where there might be interesting things happening.

"Four financial statements?" she questioned.

"Yes we will construct a Balance Sheet, an Income Statement, a Statement of Retained Earnings, and a Statement of Cash Flows."

Figure 1-11
(Left side of equal sign)

	Assets						
	Cash	A/R	Inv.	Sup.	F/A	A/D	=
0	1000	500	200	100	6000	-1600	=
1	3000						
2			4000				
3		6000					
4			-3000				
5	-2000				2000		
6	5500	-5500					
7	-2000						
8						-500	
9	-3600						
10	-200						
11	-50			50			
12	-70						
13	1580	1000	1200	150	8000	-2100	=
14							

34

"What did you say the purpose of this exercise is?" she wanted to know.

"The grid we created is a way of organizing the raw data into accounts. We had just a few transactions, but if we had thousands we might break out more accounts, but we could still collect them into some organized groupings. Now we are going to put the summarized totals into a format so we can try and make more sense about what is actually happening. We want to

Figure 1-11 (continued)
(Right side of equal sign)

Claims (Liabilities & Equity)					
A/P	N/P	LTD	C/S	R/E	Desc.
300	100	1500	4000	300	Beg Bal.
			3000		
4000					
				6000	Revenue
				-3000	C.O.G.S.
				-2000	Opr. Exp.
				-500	Dep. Exp.
-3600					
				-200	Inc. Tax
				-70	Dividend
700	100	1500	7000	530	End. Bal.

do comparisons, see relationships and be able to make some decisions."

"You said there are going to be four different statements. Why so many," she wanted to know.

"They have different purposes. The Balance Sheet is a snap shot of the business on a particular day. It shows the position of the business, how the accounts are summarized into various groupings and if the Assets equal the Claims. It usually shows a beginning balance and an ending balance. It would be just like placing two photos of you side by side, one taken last month and the other taken today."

"That is an interesting way to think about it," she noted.

"The other statements all show activity. The Income Statement reveals the results of operating the business and how the Earnings were generated."

"The Statement of Retained Earnings reconciles the change in that account. It shows the beginning balance, the increases to the account, the decreases to the account and how we got to the ending balance."

"The Statement of Cash Flows examines the change in the Cash account. What caused Cash to go up and what caused it to go down."

"It seems like Earnings and Cash are the two most important things," she interjected.

"All of the accounts are important, but they don't involve a collection of as many different types of activities as do Earnings and Cash." He paused and waited for her to ask another question, but she was quiet. "Let's start by removing the shading from the two columns for the description and the equal sign. Now I'm going to highlight with shading the Beginning Balance row and the Ending Balance Row to show that we are using these sets of numbers (Figure1-11). We are going

36

to transfer them to the Balance Sheet format (Figure 1-12)."

Figure 1-12

Balance Sheet

Assets	End. Bal.	Beg. Bal.
Cash	1580	1000
Acct. Receivable	1000	500
Inventory	1200	200
Supplies	150	100
Current Assets	3930	1800
Fixed Assets	8000	6000
Accum. Depr.	-2100	-1600
Total Assets	9830	6200

Claims		
Acct. Payable	700	300
Notes Payable	100	100
Current Liabilities	800	400
Long-term Debt	1500	1500
Total Liabilities	2300	1900
Common Stock	7000	4000
Retained Earnings	530	300
Total Liab. & Equity	9830	6200

"The Balance Sheet is structured to show liquidity. The accounts that are most liquid or nearest to being converted to cash are listed first and those that are least liquid listed last."

"We group the accounts that will be converted to cash in the next year first, summarize those and give them a title of 'Current.' Current Assets will generate positive cash in the next year, while Current Liabilities will require a payout of cash in the same time period.

"I've highlighted the numbers that are coming from the grid with the subtotals and totals remaining without shading," he noted.

"Did you use every number from those two rows on the grid?" she asked.

"I need to use every one of them so that I will balance. If you compare the Total Assets for each column on the Balance Sheet to the Total Liabilities and Equity in the same column you should see the same number. If the numbers are the same that gives us great comfort that the system is working."

She leaned in close and examined the Balance Sheet that appeared on the screen. "I think I understand."

"I've also inserted a subtotal on the Claims side for the 'Total Liabilities.' This adds the Current Liabilities to the Long-Term Debt to give me a total for all those accounts where I have an obligation to repay where credit has been extended to me. I could also have added subtotals for a lot of other groups, such as Net Fixed Assets and Stockholder's Equity, but I wanted to keep the statement relatively simple."

She continued to examine the statement as he talked.

"You will also note that I put the beginning balances in the right hand column and the ending balances to their left and closest to the descriptions."

"So does this Balance Sheet shed any light on the identity of who is really responsible for murdering Victor?" she asked with some anxiety.

"I don't know yet. I'd like to finish preparing all the statements and then try to answer that question, if you could be patient just a little while longer."

"That is one thing I have never been very good at, patience," she confessed.

"Patience is the key to almost everything," he instructed. So just hang in there a little bit. We will prepare the Income Statement next. I'm going to highlight almost all of the numbers in the R/E or Retained Earnings column: All except for the dividend number (Figure 1-13).

Figure 1-13

(Right side of equal sign)

Claims (Liabilities & Equity)					
A/P	N/P	LTD	C/S	R/E	Desc.
300	100	1500	4000	300	Beg Bal.
			3000		
4000					
				6000	Revenue
				-3000	C.O.G.S.
				-2000	Opr. Exp.
				-500	Dep. Exp.
-3600					
				-200	Inc. Tax
				-70	Dividend
700	100	1500	7000	530	End. Bal.

I will take these numbers and copy them into a format that shows Revenue minus Cost of Goods Sold to get a number that I calculate for 'Gross Profit.' From that number I will subtract the expenses to arrive at the 'E.B.I.T.' or Earnings Before Interest and Taxes. We didn't have any interest expense, so I will subtract zero to generate 'E.B.T.' or Earnings Before Taxes. Then I'll subtract the Income Taxes to get Net Income. Net Income represents the Earnings for the period (Figure 1-14)."

Figure 1-14

Income Statement

Description	Amount
Revenue	6000
Cost of Goods Sold	-3000
Gross Profit	3000
Operating Expenses	-2000
Depreciation Expense	-500
E.B.I.T.	500
Interest Expense	0
E.B.T.	500
Income Taxes	-200
Net Income	300

"It seems a little complicated. Why are there so many subtotals to get to the Earnings?"

"This is the formatting that I prefer. There are a lot of ways to structure the statement and in fact there are a lot of names that various companies apply to the statement. Not all businesses call it an Income Statement."

"Some companies call it a Statement of Operations or an Operating Statement. It can be very confusing for many people."

"I agree. Why isn't everything standard so people could more easily understand?"

"I'm not sure I know why. I have a theory that complication is a form of protection for some people. The more confusion some people can generate the less other people can understand."

"Once again the numbers transferred from the grid are shaded, while the subtotal and totals are not.

"Why didn't you transfer over the dividend amount?" she asked.

"Dividends are a payment of Earnings to the owners and not an Expense of the business. Theoretically, it comes after we have completed operations and determined if there are any Earnings. Then the owners decide if they want to take a portion of those Earnings out of the business or leave them in. If they leave them, we call that reinvesting them back into the business. Once again let me remind you that all the Earnings of the business belong to the stockholders. It is their payment for sharing their financing capital with the company."

"You make it sound like the reason the company exists is to make money for the owners and not to provide a valuable service or product to society," she challenged.

"That's why we call it Capitalism."

"I'm not so sure I like that."

"I think you have just summarized one of the great economic debates of our time. I'm going to prepare the Statement of Retained Earnings (Figure 1-15). The only box I will shade is the amount I've transferred from our grid. The Net Income amount was transferred from the Income Statement."

Figure 1-15
Statement of Retained Earnings

Description	Amount
Beginning Balance	300
Add: Net Income	300
Deduct: Dividends	-70
Ending Balance	530

"If I compare the beginning and ending balances to the grid I can see that they agree."

Cash is King

"The last financial statement we are going to create is probably my favorite. In fact it is really two statements."

"What do you mean?"

"The regulatory group that first introduced the Statement of Cash Flows wanted everyone to use a format they called the 'Direct Method.' But most companies wanted to use another approach which they called the 'Indirect Method,' so we can prepare it using either approach. I'm first going to try the Direct Method and see what we get and, then do the other and see what it generates."

She looked at him with great curiosity. "I get the sense that you are really enjoying this."

"What's not to like? A great friend I'm trying to help, a mystery to be solved, and clues everywhere we look!"

She gave him a sideways smile. "What do we do now?"

"I'm going to use all the data in the first column of the grid, the Cash account (Figure 1-16). This statement will show the cash that came in and went out of the company. We will organize it in such a way that it will focus on three functional areas: Operating activity, Investing activity, and Financing activity."

"Operating activity is the result of those cash transactions that directly affected the Earnings process. Within the Operating activity section we are going to restate the Income Statement on a cash basis. Operationally we earned Revenue, but for cash purposes we actually collected a different number. The Income Statement reflects $6,000 of revenue earned, but the cash

43

account shows that we collected $5,500 from customers for the period."

Figure 1-16

Figure 1-16
(Left side of equal sign)

	Assets						
	Cash	A/R	Inv.	Sup.	F/A	A/D	=
0	1000	500	200	100	6000	-1600	=
1	3000						
2			4000				
3		6000					
4			-3000				
5	-2000				2000		
6	5500	-5500					
7	-2000						
8						-500	
9	-3600						
10	-200						
11	-50			50			
12	-70						
13	1580	1000	1200	150	8000	-2100	=
14							

"The Income Statement shows the Cost of Goods Sold or the inventory of $3,000 delivered during the period to customers that was related to sales. If we look at the cash account we see that we paid vendors/suppliers $3,600 during the period. The Income Statement shows the earnings process and the cash account shows what we actually took in and paid out. This is operating activity

44

because it relates to the activities with customers, suppliers, and expenses of operating the business."

Figure 1-16 (continued)
(Right side of equal sign)

Claims (Liabilities & Equity)					
A/P	N/P	LTD	C/S	R/E	Desc.
300	100	1500	4000	300	Beg Bal.
			3000		
4000					
				6000	Revenue
				-3000	C.O.G.S.
				-2000	Opr. Exp.
				-500	Dep. Exp.
-3600					
				-200	Inc. Tax
				-70	Dividend
700	100	1500	7000	530	End. Bal.

"We separate this activity from Investing actions where the company purchased and sold long-term assets. Everytime the company makes an expenditure for physical or tangible assets that have a productive life of more than a year and will be used in the revenue generation process we call this Investing in the company."

These acquisitions never appear on the Income Statement, but are changes in the Fixed Assets on the Balance Sheet. Sometimes this could be for intangible assets, but that is a discussion for another time."

Figure 1-17

Statement of Cash Flows (Direct)

Description	Amount
Cash Collections	5500
Inventory Purchases	-3600
Supplies Purchases	-50
Operating Expenses	-2000
Income Taxes Paid	-200
Operating Cash Flows	-350
Fixed Asset Spending	-2000
Investing Cash Flows	-2000
Dividends Paid	-70
Common Stock Issued	3000
Financing Cash Flows	2930
Change in Cash	580
Beginning Cash Balance	1000
Ending Cash Balance	1580

"Since the company paid cash to acquire fixed assets for the period the Investing Activity will be the same as the change in the Fixed Asset account. This is not always the case."

"The last section of the Statement of Cash Flows shows the changes in the cash account as the result of financing activities for the period that relate to the claims side of the balance sheet. They are accounts that require the company to pay a cost for the use of funds."

"Accounts Payable is a working capital account and is the result of credit extended by suppliers. There is generally no cost for the use of these funds and so this account is an operating activity account. Year-end accruals are similar in nature."

"The company has obligations to those who lent it money or to those who have an ownership position through the equity accounts. So, cash transactions that affect long-term debts and common stock are shown in the Financing Activity section of the statement."

"It's getting a little complicated," she said as she shook her head from side to side.

"Let's review what I've been telling you. What are the three sections of the Statement of Cash Flows?"

"They are the Operating, Investing, and Financing sections."

"Good, and what does the Direct Method show the change in?"

"It shows all the activity in the Cash Account for the period."

"The Operating Activity section shows a restatement of what?"

"It is how the Income Statement would look if it reflected cash transactions and not earnings."

"Your Income Statement showed a positive $300 of Net Income for the period. On the other hand the Operating Cash Flow for the period was a negative $350," Nobel pointed out.

"That sounds bad."

"Well, it is not necessarily good."

"You said we were going to do the 'Direct Method' and the 'Indirect Method'."

"Both show the same results, it is how we get there that is interesting. I'm going to go back to the spreadsheet and subtract the ending balances for each account from their beginning balances.

Figure 1-18
(Left side of equal sign)

	Cash	=	A/R	Invn.	Supp.	F/A	A/D
			Claimes minus				
1	1000	=	-500	-200	-100	-6000	1600
2	3000						
3				-4000			
4			-6000				
5				3000			
6	-2000					-2000	
7	5500		5500				
8	-2000						
9							500
10	-3600						
11	-200						
12	-50				-50		
13	-70						
14	1580	=	-1000	-1200	-150	-8000	2100
15	580	=	-500	-1000	-50	-2000	500

"I will show the change in row 15. Then I'm going to subtract all of the non-cash assets from both sides of the equal sign. This effectively shows that the

48

change in cash can be explained by the change in all the other accounts. If claims go up it is a source of cash. If assets go up it is a use of cash. This is another way to look at how our change in cash can be explained (Figure 1-18).

Figure 1-18 (continued)
(Right side of equal sign)

Non-Cash Assets					
A/P	N/P	LTD	C/S	R/E	Desc.
300	100	1500	4000	300	Beg Bal.
			3000		
4000					
				6000	Revenue
				-3000	C.O.G.S.
				-2000	Opr. Exp.
				-500	Dep. Exp.
-3600					
				-200	Inc. Tax
				-70	Dividend
700	100	1500	7000	530	End. Bal.
400	0	0	3000	230	Change

"Now I'm going to use all the change amounts in the 'Indirect Method'.

Figure 1-19

Statement of Cash Flows (Indirect)

Description	Amount
Net Income	300
Depreciation Expense	500
Change in Accounts Receivable	-500
Change in Inventory	-1000
Change in Supplies	-50
Change in Accounts Payable	400
Operating Cash Flows	-350
Fixed Asset Spending	-2000
Investing Cash Flows	-2000
Dividends Paid	-70
Common Stock Issued	3000
Financing Cash Flows	2930
Change in Cash	580
Beginning Cash Balance	1000
Ending Cash Balance	1580

"I transferred all the change amounts from row 15 to the Statement of Cash Flows for the Indirect Method. As you can see the Investing and Financing Cash Flows are the same for either the Direct or Indirect methods. What changed was the Operating Cash Flow detail while the subtotal stayed the same (Figure 1-19)."

"In the Indirect Method we will show a reconciliation of the Net Income to the Operating Cash Flow. We start with Net Income, add back Depreciation

Expense and then add or subtract all the changes to the Current Asset and Current Liability accounts."

"I don't understand. Why do you show the Change in Accounts Receivable as a negative when in fact the balance went up on the Balance Sheet?"

"When Accounts Receivable goes up, it means we did not collect the cash and so reflects negatively on the Cash account. In the same fashion, when Inventory goes up it also is tying up cash and so reduces our cash account."

"But when Accounts Payable goes up it represents positive cash flow, so how does that work?"

"By increasing Accounts Payable we are not paying out cash," he offered.

She thought about it for a moment and then said, "I think I get it."

"This is probably the best statement for offering us some clues. I have some questions for you," he posed.

"I'll answer them if I can."

"The company has a negative cash flow from operations, but reported a positive Net Income. It looks like the problem is in the Accounts Receivable and Inventory areas."

She looked at the statement, "Particularly in the Inventory area."

"Can you think of any reason why the company would be building up Inventory?"

"Not really," she confessed.

"Also, with Accounts Receivable going up, do you have any reason to believe that some of the reported sales might be bogus?"

"What do you mean bogus?"

"Could you be reporting Revenue that is not real and simply fictitious to make the Earnings look good?"

"Wow, I don't know."

"From my perspective we have three areas to really focus on. First, we need to evaluate the large issuance of stock this period to some mystery person and the related payment of dividends. Second, we should look at the purchase of Inventory and see if that is an arm's length transaction. Third, we should see what the mark-up is and if the sales are legitimate."

"How do we do all that?"

"Is your company closed today?"

"There are several people who come in on Saturdays, if that is what you want to know."

"Hum, do you have access to the accounting office?"

"I have a master key to the building. What about tonight? We can go after dark, say about ten. I'll drive," she offered.

"That sounds good," he responded.

Surprise Visitor

After she left, he spent the rest of the day working hard in his yard. All the time, his mind was filled with thoughts of her, the murder, the clues, and seeing her again late that evening. He was filled with great anticipation, and yet he knew that the best cure for impatience was to do something else in the meantime.

Working so hard in the yard all day long had made him physically tired by the time evening came. He looked at his watch and it was eight-thirty. Putting his tools away in the shed, he went into the house and up to his room on the second floor. He removed his work clothes, showered, and had just pulled his pants on when he heard the back door open and close.

He froze and remembered that when he came in he hadn't locked the door. Listening very quietly, he heard someone come up the back stairs to the kitchen. Then he heard noises from the kitchen and he moved to the landing overlooking the hallway that led to the kitchen door.

Suddenly, the light in the kitchen went on and Hannah came walking through the door. She was carrying a basket of bread, stopped, looked up at him and said, "Where do you want to eat? Oh, I hope you don't mind. I've noticed you working so hard all day long and decided to sacrifice for a friend. I've made dinner."

He pointed through another door. "In there is the dining room, but why don't we just eat in the kitchen, if that is okay. I'll finish dressing." He turned and retreated back into his room.

As they were finishing dinner he asked, "That was excellent so now tell me a little more about what the company does and who you suspect."

"We sell retail pet Supplies, but we mostly contract with large corporate accounts like zoos and such. The three people I suspect most would be Woodrow Peck, head of sales, Margaret Pie, head of accounting, and Humperdinck Bird, head of production. Any of them could be involved in the issuance of new stock. Peck or Pie I suspect could be behind the increase in Accounts Receivable and Bird may have something to do with the build-up in Inventory. Then again, it could be any of them," she concluded.

He looked out the window and then at his watch. "It's dark now, why don't we head for the office."

When they arrived at the office the blackness of the night engulfed them. She parked down the street and they walked to the building. As she was unlocking the back door, she paused. "Did you hear that?"

He listed, "I don't hear anything."

"I heard something," she said as she paused a bit longer and then pushed the door open and they entered. She pulled a small flashlight from her purse and clicked it on. "What are we looking for?"

"We need to get to the accounting records."

"This way," she said and led them forward. They came to the locked door of an office in a far corner. "I don't know if my key will get us in here. Wow, it does," she said with some surprise. She moved to one corner as he hurried quickly to the desk and began searching the drawers. He turned on the computer and as he waited for it to boot up he searched for keys that would unlock various filing cabinets that lined one wall.

He noticed a small area rug in front of the desk and one corner appeared to be rumpled. He lifted it and found two keys. He handed them to Hannah, "You go through those drawers and look for copies of invoices and purchase orders," he instructed.

Back at the computer he searched the icons for files and folders on the screen. "I'm not sure if I can get anything out of this, and we will need passwords to get into anything that will really do us any good."

"I don't know if this will help," she said standing in front of an open file drawer and holding a folder open. She handed it over and he examined it.

"These are copies of your invoices billing for products that have been shipped. It looks like you are charging $75 per 100 pounds of exotic bird seed. Do you see a folder for purchase orders?" he said as the light of the computer screen illuminated his face and the documents he was examining.

She directed the flashlight across the various folders. "Here it is." She handed the folder to him.

He scanned the pages in the folder. "It appears that you are paying $50 for the same 100 pounds of exotic bird seed."

"What does that mean?" she asked.

"On first blush, it looks like you are adding a 50% mark-up on products sold, at least on this item." He quickly reviewed other pages from both folders. "It looks like that is pretty consistent."

"I still don't get it," she confessed.

"The entry we made into the grid for Revenue was $6,000 and the related delivery of Inventory was for $3,000. That is a one hundred percent mark-up, not fifty percent."

"So, what does that mean?"

"I think someone may be padding the Revenue to make the financial statements look good."

"Oh, that is terrible. We may be in deep financial trouble and not know it."

"That's right. In addition to that you have a large build-up of Inventory that is potentially not going to be sold. That would mean more losses for the company. Look and see if you can find a file with stockholder information."

After examining all the folders in that drawer, she closed it and began going through other drawers. He continued to struggle with the computer, trying to access information that could help.

"I think I've got it, look here!" she exclaimed. She handed him a folder and he read the tab that said 'stock certificates.'

"I didn't know anyone still issued certificates," he said as he opened the file. "Well, there are no real certificates in here, but there is a listing of what stock was issued, the date and to whom. That last certificate for 3,000 shares went to…" he stopped reading abruptly as the sound of a wastebasket being kicked over echoed from the offices outside where they were.

"Someone is out there," she whispered as she clicked off her flashlight.

He put his forefinger to his lips to signal for her to be quiet.

Reconciliation

They froze, silently listening and then heard the sound of someone entering the office next to where they were.

The two individuals in the accounting office slowly moved to the door they had come in through. Hannah slowly opened the door and peered out into the large open area where several desks were clustered in the middle. They eased their way out of the office and as they did noticed the door to the next office was closed, but the light of a flashlight danced on the floor beneath it.

They moved to the cluster of desks and then heard a door begin to open. They crouched down behind one of the desks as a man came out of the office, turned and went to the accounting office. He pushed the door open, stepped in, and looked around quickly searching for the reason the computer screen was on. Then he wheeled and scanned the open area.

Hannah jumped up and began to run for the front door. Noble immediately followed her. Taken aback by the sudden burst, the intruder was caught by surprise. He hesitated only a few seconds, but was soon giving chase.

The front door jammed. Hannah turned and was off leading the trio down a long hallway. At the end she bolted to the left and up a flight of stairs to a landing and through a door onto the roof.

The roof was a large flat area with trellises, birdhouses and statuary for the demonstration of bird related products. Hannah dodged in and out of the maze toward a far ledge where an iron fire escape led over and down to the ground.

As Hannah and Noble approached the escape, the man following them had closed the distance and cut them off. He jumped in front of them and they froze. He was holding a gun.

"So it is you, Woodrow. You're the one who killed Victor and have tried to frame me. You are the one who has been padding the Revenue to make the company look better than it really is."

"That's right, and you are the one who coerced the company to issue stock to you so you could take the company over once the two principals were out of the way," Noble added.

"I'm sorry to hear that you have figured it all out. You probably know that I have a life insurance policy on the owners that will set me up with millions. Now if you two love birds will accommodate me and commit suicide by jumping to your deaths, everything will be fine."

Just then Hannah's accomplice raised his right arm above the head of the gunman and began to draw it across from left to right and as he did said, "Balance Sheet." Then he lowered it a bit and drawing it across from left to right again said, "Balance Sheet."

The gunman looked on in confusion as though he were watching an Indian medicine man inscribe an oath to some god. "What are you doing?" he cursed.

The friend then placed his hand high to the right and lowering it said, "Income Statement." Then to the left in a parallel fashion lowered it saying, "Statement of Cash Flows."

As he dropped his hand with the gunman's eyes glued to the motion, Hannah swung the bag she was carrying as hard as she could and caught the gunman squarely on the side of the head. He fell like a load of bricks and was unconscious with the gun lying beside him.

"That flashlight must be heavy," she offered.

"We know he's the murderer and he knows he's the murderer, but how do we convince the authorities of the truth? We have a paper trail that supports motive, but it still might be a challenge."

"I don't think so," Hannah announced as she produced a cell phone. "I have recorded everything."

"How beautifully simple," was all he could say.

Summary of Concepts

2/10, net 30: If you pay in ten days you can deduct 2% as a discount, but if not then you will pay the full amount in 30 days.

Accounts Payable: Accounts Payable are the result of the business purchasing Inventory and/or Supplies from vendors, who have a Claim on the Assets of the business as long as their account goes unpaid.

Accounts Receivable: Accounts Receivable are like a stack of IOUs from customers. They have value, and in fact can be sold to a bank or collection agency for money.

Accumulated Depreciation: Accumulated Depreciation is what we call a contra-Asset. It shows how much of Fixed Assets or equipment have been consumed over the life of the Asset. When we subtract the Accumulated Depreciation amount from the Fixed Asset amount we find what we call the Net Value of the Fixed Assets.

Assets and Claims: I have two groups of accounts. The group in the left are Assets and the group on the right I've labeled Claims.

Assets: Assets are things of value the company owns and uses to make the business operate.

Balance Sheet: The Balance Sheet is a snapshot of the business on a particular day. It shows the position of the business, how the accounts are summarized into various groupings and if the Assets equal the Claims.

Balance: The equal sign is extremely important. It is the one thing that is absolute in accounting. The Assets must equal the Claims.

Capitalism: The reason the company exists is to make money for the owners and not to provide a valuable service or product to society. That's why we call it capitalism.

Claims: Everything on the right side of the equal sign shows who has a Claim on the Assets of the business.

Common Stock: When someone purchases an ownership position in a business they can be issued stock certificates that represent their share of the equity Claim. They give money to the business to use in return for a promise to receive all the Earnings of the business.

Cost of Goods Sold: When Inventory is delivered to the customer, an Asset is reduced and goes out of the business. This reduces the Earnings of the business and is recorded as Cost of Goods Sold in the Retained Earnings account.

Current Accounts: Current Assets will generate positive cash in the next year, while Current Liabilities will require a payout of cash in the same time period.

Dividends: Dividends are a payment of Earnings to the owners and not an expense of the business.

Double Entry System: The double entry system means that every time the business records a transaction they must make at least two entries. Assets must always equal the Claims.

E.B.I.T.: The Earnings Before Interest and Taxes is the Gross Profit minus all the operating expenses.

E.B.T.: Earnings Before Taxes is the E.B.I.T. less any interest expense.

Equality: If you compare the Total Assets for each column on the Balance Sheet to the Total Liabilities and Equity in the same column, you should see the same number.

Financing Activity: Financing activity is the result of the company receiving or paying principle and interest on debt in addition to receiving or distributing money to and from the stockholders and any related dividends.

Gross Profit: Revenue minus Cost of Goods Sold is the Gross Profit.

Income Statement: The Income Statement reveals the results of operating the business and how the Earnings were generated.

Investing Activity: Investing activity is the result of purchasing or selling Long-Term Assets for the business.

Liquidation: If the company was to go out of business and the Assets had to be liquidated or converted to cash, the money generated would be given to everyone who has a Claim.

Liquidity: The Balance Sheet is structured to show liquidity. The accounts that are most liquid or nearest to being converted to cash are listed first and those that are furthest away listed last.

Long-Term Debts: This is a Claim by people or banks who have lent money to the business. The company agrees to repay the amount at a specified period of time, plus interest for the use of the money. It is usually for several years.

Net Income: Subtract Income Taxes from E.B.T. to get Net Income. Net Income represents the Earnings for the period.

Notes Payable: Companies go to a bank and agree to get a short-term loan to carry them over for a few months. They sign a note and show it on their books as a Note Payable to the bank.

Operating Cash Flows (Direct Method): The first section of the Statement of Cash Flows is a recasting of the Income Statement on a totally cash basis.

Operating Cash Flows (Indirect Method): This will show a reconciliation of the Net Income to the Operating Cash Flow. We start with Net Income, add back Depreciation Expense and then add or subtract all the changes to the Current Asset and Current Liability accounts.

Retained Earnings: Earnings that are left in the business for growth instead of paid out to the owners is Retained Earnings. This is like an Accounts Payable to the owners and increases their Claim.

Revenue: When we sell products it is like we are getting a big bucket of Earnings that belong to the stock holders. We record this in Retained Earnings.

Spreadsheets: A spreadsheet is a grid of rows and columns where we can enter words, amounts, formulas, or references. It will help us organize the data.

Statement of Cash Flows: The Statement of Cash Flows examines the change in the cash account, what caused cash to go up and what caused it to go down.

Statement of Retained Earnings: The Statement of Retained Earnings reconciles the change in that account. It shows the beginning balance, the increases to the account, the decreases to the account and how we got to the ending balance.

Tangible Assets: Cash, Inventory, Supplies, and Fixed Assets are all tangible Assets.

Total Liabilities: This is the sum of Current Liabilities and Long-Term Debt.

RISKY

Learning Objectives

An understanding of:
Time Value of Money
Present Value
Future Value
Annuity Payments
Rate of Return
Constant Growth
Perpetuity
Horizon Value
Uneven Cash Flows

Spreadsheet Tools found at
www.businessallstars.com/calculator

Assessment found at
www.businessallstars.com/assessment

Detective Hammersmith

Nobel found his car at the airport, paid the fee and drove home. It had been a long flight and it was late in the day as he pulled into his driveway. The garage door slowly rose and he pulled in. After retrieving his bags from the trunk he turned and saw Hannah, his next door neighbor, standing in the middle of the driveway, just outside the garage. She looked the picture of perfection, but had a serious look on her face.

"Hannah, what is it?"

"First let me say, welcome back. Was the flight long and tiring?"

"I was able to get some sleep, but I'm still weary. You look troubled. Is everything alright?"

"Your fame is beginning to spread as a creative problem solver. Detective Hammersmith from the homicide division came by to see you while you were gone and I happened to catch him, since I've been keeping a lookout on your house while you were gone. I took the opportunity to find out what he wanted."

"Is he the same guy that was involved in your case?"

"That's right, and now he wants to consult with you regarding a case he is having problems with."

"Oh dear, this sounds serious."

Nobel was holding a suit case in his right hand as he closed the trunk with his left. Hannah approached and picked up the travel bag that was resting at his feet. "Maybe we should go inside," she instructed.

"Good idea."

They carried the bags into Nobel's house where he sat down on the couch in the sitting room and placed his bag on the floor beside him. Hannah set his travel bag down and asked: "Do you want something to drink?"

"Sure, a glass of water would be great."

Hannah went to the kitchen and returned with two glasses of water. "Are you sure this is all you want? By the way, how did the seminar go?"

"It is always hard to know. I think it went well. But when you are talking about global concepts the participants always need a lot of examples to make sense of anything. Do you remember the Statement of Cash Flow that we developed for your company?"

"Yes, I think so."

"It was divided into the Operating, Investing and Financing sections. I tried to show how most financial decisions within a company are divided into those same three areas."

"Were you effective?"

"I'm not sure. What do you think I should do about this Detective Hammersmith thing?"

Hannah pulled from the pocket of her jeans a folded up newspaper clipping and handed it to Nobel. "I wonder if it is about this. I had to go back and search the papers for the last several seeks and finally found what I though was an unsolved murder."

Nobel examined the article and then read aloud: "Prominent investment-fund partner found dead. Halley Strong was found dead in her home after an apparent overdose of drugs early Saturday morning. She had entertained several employees in her home the night before and was found by a friend the next morning who came to pick her up for a planned outing. When there was no response, the friend entered the home and found Halley in her bedroom. The police are investigating the possibility of foul play, but suicide has not been ruled out." Nobel paused and then added, "How interesting. I wonder why Hammersmith wants to see me."

"He said there is a financial aspect of this case that you may be able to shed some light on."

"Well, I will certainly be glad to help. By the way, what is the status of your business?"

"I don't really think I'm cut out to run the business and so I've decided to sell it."

"Are you going to return to modeling?"

"I'm not sure. By the way..." she pulled from another pocket a slip of paper and handed it to Nobel. "This is Hammersmith's number."

"I guess I'd better call him as soon as possible." Nobel entered the number in his phone and waited. "Hello, is this detective Hammersmith? This is Nobel Merchant. I understand you want to see me...yes....yes....yes...that will be fine."

"What did he say?" Hannah was impatient.

"He is going to come by at ten tomorrow morning."

"Do you mind if I tag along?" Hannah asked.

Nobel looked a little puzzled, but then responded. "Sure, why not?"

The Set-up

Hannah knocked on the front door at exactly nine-forty-five. Nobel greeted her and welcomed her in. "This is really exciting," she said.

"I'm glad someone is getting some enjoyment out of this. I feel a little under the gun. I'm not sure exactly what to expect, but feel some pressure to deliver for the detective."

"You will do great. Maybe that is why I'm here, to give you the moral support you need."

At ten o'clock an unmarked police car pulled up in front of Nobel's home, two people got out of the car and walked to the front door. Before they could knock, Hannah opened the door and welcomed them in.

"Hello, do you remember me? I'm Detective Hammersmith and this is Sergeant Rice," a tall gentleman said as he introduced his female companion.

"Come into the sitting room and have a seat," Nobel instructed.

When they were all seated Hannah spoke up. "My name is Hannah Watson, I live next door, and you can call me Watson," she offered with a smile.

Hammersmith turned to Nobel. "I'm sure you are wondering what I want. Well, about two weeks ago a woman was murdered in her home. Her name was Halley Strong."

Nobel produced the newspaper clipping and handed it to the detective. "Is that her? Hannah found it in the paper. I thought the article said you were unsure if it was foul-play or suicide."

"Oh, it was murder alright, but we didn't want the press to give our hand away. We have narrowed the suspects down to the four people who were at her home the night before. They were all people who worked for her and were in line to succeed to a partner position in the firm. There are two women and two men: Keri Omar, Lara Pullman, Mark Martinez, and Nick Wang. We are sure it had to be one of them. The only problem is we can't close the deal and identify which it was."

"How can I help?" Nobel wondered.

"The firm they all work in is an investment firm and we need someone with some knowledge of these things. I was quite impressed how you helped Ms. Watson here and when your name came to me, I knew you were the one I needed."

"I'll be glad to help if I can."

"We don't have many clues, but there is one that we don't know what to do with." Hammersmith handed a picture to Nobel.

"We think Halley scrawled this in salt on her table just before she died. We're not sure what to make of it. It looks like a capital B, but none of the suspects have that letter in their name. We have checked their offices, homes, and anything else we can think of, but have drawn a blank."

"Very interesting," Nobel said as he examined the figure. As he studied it, Hannah left her chair and leaned in close so she could study the image also.

"Do you have any idea what it could mean?" the female officer asked.

"I might. Do all of these individuals know they are suspects?" Nobel asked.

"They probably do, but we are playing suicide up to try and get them to lower their guard."

"I have an idea how we could potentially trap the criminal, but I would need cooperation from Halley's partner at the investment firm."

"I don't think that's any problem."

"Good. What is that individual's name?"

"Peter Weinberger," Sgt. Rice replied.

"This will be a risky effort, but I think it just might work. Will you tell Mr. Weinberger that I will contact him tomorrow morning and lay out my plan?"

"Certainly, is there anything you would like to tell us?" Hammersmith asked.

"I would rather reserve my plan until it unfolds and see if it works, if that's alright."

"I'm willing to trust you," said the detective.

When the detective and sergeant had gone, Hannah asked, "I'm not sure I understand."

"I'm going to try and expose the murderer using a time value of money model."

"Could you explain it to me?"

"Let me give you a few of the basics. There is a spreadsheet model that calculates the present value of future cash flows. It takes those cash flows and brings them back to the present using a discount rate. It is based on a very simple concept. Nobel opened his laptop and brought up the model (Figure 2-1).

Figure 2-1
(Left side of excel worksheet)

TVM = Time V

Copyright © 20013 ACB
BusinessAll

Name

Standard Four Function Calculator		
S	Inputs	Results
Rate - Interest Rate		
Nper - Number of Periods		
FV - Future Value		
PV - Present Value		
Pmt - Annuity Payment		
Type - Begin = 1; End = 0	0	

Discount Rate	
Growth Rate	
Net Present Value	$0.00

"It looks complicated," Hannah mused.

"It is based on a very simple formula. If you put $100 in a bank account that earns 10% interest, how much money will you have at the end of one year?"

"That is pretty easy, I will have $110."

"How did you arrive at that figure?"

"I simply multiplied the original $100 by 10% and added the $10 to the original amount."

"That is the time value of money concept explained as well as anybody could. I can put that into a mathematical formula, but don't panic."

Figure 2-1 (continued)
(Right side of excel worksheet)

alue of Money

A - All Rights Reserved
stars.com

| | | | Date | |

H	Year	Cash Flows	Specific Cash Flows Discounted		Total FV
	0		$	-	$ -
	1				$ -
	2				$ -
	3				$ -
	4				$ -
	5				$ -
	6				$ -
	7				$ -
	8				$ -
	9				$ -
	10				$ -
	11				$ -

"I'll try not to."

"We say that the future value or FV is equal to the present value PV times itself plus the rate of interest.

$$FV = PV \times (1 + r)$$

"We multiply the present value times itself to bring the original amount forward and add it to the

73

interest we have earned. We wouldn't want to only show the resulting interest without the starting amount."

"That seems pretty simple."

"It is the basic building block of finance. If I was going to leave the money in the bank for three years and then find how much I had I would multiply the present value by one plus the interest rate three times:

$$FV = PV \times (1 + r) \times (1 + r) \times (1 + r)$$

"The results would tell me how much I would have in the bank at the end of three years. Rather than stringing long sequences of the same thing together I can write the formula as:

$$FV = PV \times (1 + r)^3$$

"Okay," Hannah concluded.

"If you look at the model there are three quantities that are represented by FV, PV, r, and the exponent, in this case 3. FV is the value at the end of the time period, PV is the value today, r is the rate of interest and the exponent is the number of periods."

"I was always pretty good at math and this seems pretty straight forward," Hannah noted.

"In finance we can compare several options with calculations like this but they may all have different time frames. One might be two years, another three years and a third five years. If we applied the formula we would end up with future values that are really not very comparable. So the trick is to bring them all back to the present so we are comparing each in today's dollars."

"That sounds reasonable, but how do you do that with this formula?"

"Suppose someone will give me $110 at the end of one year. How much is that worth today? Remember the original calculation where we multiplied a base amount of $100 times itself plus the interest rate to get $110. Can we reverse the process?"

"I'm not sure."

"It is simple. We just divide each side of the equal sign by the $(1 + r)$ factor that cancels it out on the right side and shows it on the left side as:

$$FV / (1 + r)^1 = PV$$

"Suppose I had a whole series of projected future cash flows and wanted to bring them all back to the present. I could apply this formula to each one of them and find their present value. When I added all the present values up, I would have a total value today for all the future cash flows."

"How interesting," Hannah seemed to get it.

"You said you want to sell your business. All we would have to do is project what your future cash flows from the business would be, find the present value for each one of them, add them up and arrive at a total value for the business."

"That would be great."

"Sometime those future cash flows are a series of routine payments that are the same for each period. We call that an annuity. Other times those future cash flows are different for each period, and we call that an uneven stream of cash flows," Nobel explained.

"That could take a lot of calculating."

"That is where the spreadsheet model comes in handy. The portion on the left has six inputs. We can enter an x to the left of the row we want to find the value for, and by entering data in all the other input cells we can get the answer.

Nobel entered an x to the left of "PV – Present Value" and then entered data in each of the input cells for the other rows. "This 'Standard Four Function Calculator' will find the present value of $100 received at the end of ten periods with an interest rate of 5%. It will also find the present value of an annuity of $10 received for each of the ten periods and discount those back at the same 5%. It will add up the two and the total is $138.61."

"Why is the answer negative?"

Figure 2-2
(Left side of excel worksheet)

TVM = Time V
Copyright © 20013 ACB
BusinessAll

Name	

Standard Four Function Calculator		
S	Inputs	Results
Rate - Interest Rate	5.00%	
Nper - Number of Periods	10	
FV - Future Value	$ 100.00	
x PV - Present Value		($138.61)
Pmt - Annuity Payment	$ 10.00	
Type - Begin = 1; End = 0	0	

Discount Rate	5.00%
Growth Rate	0.00%
Net Present Value	$138.61

"The way the computer is programed it assumes that some dollars will be going out and others will be coming in. Since I entered the inputs as positive it assumed they were dollars that were coming to me and so the answer is negative to show the present value must be negative or going out to offset it."

"This little box works great where we have a single sum and/or an annuity, but if we have an uneven stream of cash flows then we have to enter each one of those individually. To do this we have the right side of the spreadsheet model. Let's enter $10 in each of the first nine rows and $110 in the ten to mirror the data from the

Figure 2-2 (continued)
(Right side of excel worksheet)

alue of Money

A - All Rights Reserved

stars.com

		Date	

		Specific Cash Flows Discounted	
H Year	Cash Flows		Total FV
0	$ -	$	-
1	$ 10.00	$	10.00
2	$ 10.00	$	10.00
3	$ 10.00	$	10.00
4	$ 10.00	$	10.00
5	$ 10.00	$	10.00
6	$ 10.00	$	10.00
7	$ 10.00	$	10.00
8	$ 10.00	$	10.00
9	$ 10.00	$	10.00
10	$ 110.00	$	110.00
11		$	-

'Standard Four Function Calculator.' We will also enter a Discount Rate and Growth Rate in the extension to the bottom left. You will see the resulting Net Present Value of the uneven stream of cash flows is the same as the present value for the annuity and future single sum from the smaller box."

Without Compounding

"I want to mention one other concept. If you leave an investment of $100 in a bank account indefinitely and take the return out every period and don't reinvest it, how much will you receive every period?"

"That is easy," Hanna responded. "You will get $10.

"We can write an equation for that never-ending cash-flow from the investment:

$$\$10 = 10\% * \$100 \quad \text{or} \quad CF = r * PV$$

"We can restate that as a present value formula for a perpetual cash-flow with a stated return:

$$\$100 = \$10 / 10\% \quad \text{or} \quad PV = CF / r$$

With Compounding

"So you can say the present value of $10 received indefinitely, given a ten percent return is $100. Now suppose that perpetual cash-flow were to increase by some constant growth rate of say 5%. What would that do to the present value of those cash-flows? Well, we can simply modify our formula by subtracting the 5% growth from the return rate in the denominator:

$$\$200 = \$10 / (10\% - 5\%) \quad \text{or} \quad PV = CF / (r - g)$$

"This is a 'Horizon Value' calculation. It is used all the time in finance and is one of the more valuable formulas."

Hannah sat mulling over all they had covered and then said: "Do you mind if I ask a crazy questions?"

"Go ahead."

"How is all this going to show who murdered that poor woman?"

"You need to be patient and everything will be revealed. I first need to meet with the other partner tomorrow. What was his name?"

"Peter Weinberger," Hannah responded. "What time do we meet with him?"

"What do you mean we?"

"I'm in this thing now and I want to see it through. You're not going to get rid of me very easily. I'm beginning to like all this finance stuff. Who knows my next career may be in the finance industry."

The Contest

Nobel and Hannah arrived at Peter's office bright and early the next morning. He was waiting for them. Introductions followed and then Peter offered: "I'm interested to see what direction you take this case."

"I may be going out on a limb, but I have an idea how we can trap the murderer," Nobel responded.

"I'll be glad to help in any way I can."

"I would like you to propose a simple contest to the four suspects. This will be a way for you to determine who the next person promoted to partner will be. Call all four of them into your office and say that you have just received a $200,000 cash deposit from a client and would like each of them to propose where to invest the sum. They will have twenty-four hours to respond and are to be back in your office one day later."

"That sounds very intriguing. I would be glad to do that. When shall we start?"

"As soon as possible," Nobel replied.

Hannah sat quietly at Nobel's, side and said nothing, but took everything in.

"Do you have a conference room?"

"Yes, it is a very nice facility."

"Good, on the day they report to you, Hannah and I will be in the conference room. They will come in and make their presentations one at a time. Detective Hammersmith and Sergeant Rice will be in an office nearby. Do you have facilities so they can listen in?"

"We do."

"Good," Nobel said enthusiastically.

"I'll get right on it," Weinberger concluded.

The Suspects

Nobel, Hannah and Peter were seated on one side of the conference room table. It was a large room with a beautiful inlaid wooden table that glistened from a polished surface. John Rowley, Peter's assistant, was standing on the opposite side of the table awaiting instructions.

"They are all in their offices, waiting instructions on when to present," John said.

"That's great." Peter leaned over to a small black device located in the middle of the table in front of them and pressed a black button. "Are you there Detective?"

From a hidden speaker a voice responded, "We are here and very interested."

"Good," Nobel replied. "If this goes at is should we will know who the murder is at the conclusion of the four presentations. I will inform you which one it is, so be ready."

"Right," came a voice from the device.

Nobel nodded to Peter who turned to John and said: "Let's begin with Keri Omar. Would you invite her to come in and make her presentation?"

In a few minutes a smartly dressed young woman was standing before them. She was introduced to the group and informed that Nobel and Hannah were the potential investors.

Very calmly she began and said that with a lump sum of $200,000 she would advise putting it all into a pool of corporate bonds with five year maturities. The pool would include a hand-selected mix of triple-A bonds, double-A, single-A, and triple-B bonds, all investment grade. The average coupon rate on this portfolio would be 5% and these bonds could be purchased at a discount and paying $230,000 on maturity.

This would result in a yield-to-maturity of 6.1053%. She said she was not sure of the exact expectation of the investors, but this conservative strategy would provide safety and a reasonable return.

She expressed appreciation for the opportunity to offer her services and hoped they would find her approach reasonable. Peter thanked her and excused her.

Nobel entered the data into the left side of his spreadsheet:

Figure 2-3
(Left side of excel worksheet)

TVM = Time V		
Copyright © 20013 ACE		
BusinessAI		

Name		

Standard Four Function Calculator		
S	Inputs	Results
Rate - Interest Rate	6.1053%	
Nper - Number of Periods	5	
FV - Future Value	$ 230,000.00	
x PV - Present Value		($200,000.48)
Pmt - Annuity Payment	$ 6,900.00	
Type - Begin = 1; End = 0	0	

Discount Rate	
Growth Rate	
Net Present Value	$0.00

"So explain this to me," Hannah queried.

"Well, we will receive $230,000 worth of face value bonds that will repay that amount on maturity in

five years. I enter that in the future value. I can find the
present value of that lump sum payment in today's
dollars by applying the formula:

$$FV / (1 + r)^t = PV$$
or
$$\$230,000.00 / (1 + .061053)^5 = \$171,018.25$$

"The bonds pay a five percent coupon rate on
those $230,000 bonds or $6,900 each year. That is an
annuity and I enter that as the payment. I find the present
value of that annuity by applying the formula to each of
those amounts:

$$\$6,900.00 / (1 + .061053)^1 = \$6,502.97$$
$$\$6,900.00 / (1 + .061053)^2 = \$6,128.79$$
$$\$6,900.00 / (1 + .061053)^3 = \$5,776.14$$
$$\$6,900.00 / (1 + .061053)^4 = \$5,443.78$$
$$\$6,900.00 / (1 + .061053)^5 = \$5,130.55$$

"The total of all the present values for the interest
payments is $28,982.23. If I add that amount to the
present value of the lump sum $171,018.25 the result is
$200,000.48. In other words I can invest $200,000 today,
receive $6,900 every year for five years and then receive
$230,000. I will be earning 6.1053% on this investment."

"I think I get it, but tell me this, is Keri the one?"
Hannah puzzled.

"Yes, what do you think?" added Peter.

"We need to hear all of them before we can tell."

John came into the room and asked: "Are you
ready for Lara?"

Peter looked at Nobel who gave a nod and Peter
returned the nod to John. Lara Pullman was a tall woman,
a bit older than Keri but still with a very professional

style. Peter introduced everyone and instructed Lara to make her pitch.

Lara explained that the firm needed to begin taking a more aggressive attitude toward the markets. One way to do this was to look at various venture capital opportunities. There were a lot of small companies who were looking for financing and would be willing to go the venture capital route. She had reviewed several of these and found one that was perfect for such an investment. It made a home medical monitor that connected to a computer program and provided the user with excellent health data on a daily basis.

She explained there were a couple of larger venture capital funds who were looking at this company as an investment and would be willing to let Lara in for a piece of the action. The annual return would be in the neighborhood of 50% per year. There would be no dividends or returns for the first five years, but then the target company would be sold off and return $1,518,750 on the original $200,000 investment.

"This would be a whole new direction for our company. We have never been involved in the venture capital market before. Are you sure we want to go in that direction?" Peter asked.

"I think is time we became more aggressive. There are many investment houses dealing in hedge funds, derivatives, and venture capital situations that are passing us by," Lara offered.

Peter sat for a long moment and then turned to Nobel. "It all sounds pretty amazing," he said. Peter thanked Lara for coming and making a rather dynamic presentation.

Once Lara was gone, Peter turned to Nobel, "I never expected that. Lara has been here a long time and I guess she just felt it was time to pull a rabbit out of the hat."

"This one seems to be pretty straight forward in terms of the calculation, but boy those numbers are amazing," Hannah noted.

Nobel entered the numbers in his spreadsheet model:

Figure 2-4
(Left side of excel worksheet)

		TVM = Time V
		Copyright © 20013 ACB
		BusinessAll

Name | |

Standard Four Function Calculator		
S	Inputs	Results
Rate - Interest Rate	50.0%	
Nper - Number of Periods	5	
FV - Future Value	$ 1,518,750.00	
x PV - Present Value		($200,000.00)
Pmt - Annuity Payment	$ -	
Type - Begin = 1; End = 0	0	

Discount Rate	
Growth Rate	
Net Present Value	$0.00

"There is no annuity, only a lump sum at the end. You are right, it is just the future value of $1,518,750 divided by one plus the fifty percent to the fifth power."

"Are we ready for the next one?" Peter asked.

"Sure," Nobel responded.

Peter nodded to John who opened the door and showed Mark Martinez into the room. Once again introductions were made and Mark was instructed to begin.

Mark began by cautioning the group that what he was about to present was a little unusual, but he felt it had real merit. A professional contact of his was the chief executive officer (CEO) of a local company that was looking to expand into the graphic imaging business. They wanted to purchase a $200,000 piece of hardware that would have a five year life and then be obsolete. During its life it would be able to generate significant revenue and as a result handsome returns.

If the $200,000 was made available to this company, the cash-flow from the project to the investors would be: $20,000; $50,000; $80,000; $90,000; and $60,000 for the five year period. Mark said that he felt very comfortable about the safety of the investment and that he personally knew the individuals involved and they were of the highest integrity and capability. He had explored the industry and the particular piece of hardware and it was well regarded with a solid track record.

"This would be handled in the form of a loan to the company secured by the machine and stock in the company," Mark noted.

"How many of these types of transactions have we done in the past? I'm not aware of any, but perhaps you did some with Halley," Peter questioned.

"I've taken several of these to Halley over the last three years since I've been with the firm and she has always steered away from them suggesting they were not the line of business we are in. I wonder if it is now time we took a closer look at these types of investments," Mark pitched.

Peter thanked Mark for his effort and excused him from the room. He then turned to Nobel and said, "Well, I'm convinced that Mark is our man."

"Are you suggesting that Mark is the murderer?" Nobel asked.

"I think so. He came to us three years ago and has always been a little different. He comes up with unusual projects and ideas. He is a bit of loner and now he wants us to invest with some guy in a local company. It all smells like trouble to me."

"So you are basing this on the fact that he is a little different in his work habits?" Hannah protested.

"Yes, and the fact that he never would go out with us for drinks after work. He's just not a team player."

"What about Keri or Lara?" Hannah continued.

"Keri is a real company person. She goes out for drinks, she always comes up with suggestions that are right down the line, and she is warm and engaging. Lara will occasionally throw out an idea that's a little off the wall, like today. But I have a lot of confidence in her judgment and ability. She has been here a long time and really paid her dues. No I think it is Mark."

Suddenly from the intercom on the table detective Hammersmith spoke up. "I've been in the business a long time, and you can never tell from the things you have just been discussing. We have been over this ground several times and I wonder what Nobel thinks."

"I think we need to hear them all out."

"That's good enough for me. Why don't we continue?" the detective offered.

"I suppose that's fair, but don't be surprised if I'm right," Peter reconciled.

"Before we continue could you explain this last calculation for me?" Hannah addressed Nobel.

"Sure."

Nobel entered the numbers into his spreadsheet model:

Figure 2-5
(Left side of excel worksheet)

TVM = Time V

Copyright © 20013 ACB

BusinessAll

Name

Standard Four Function Calculator		
S	Inputs	Results
Rate - Interest Rate		
Nper - Number of Periods		
FV - Future Value		
PV - Present Value		
Pmt - Annunity Payment	$ -	
Type - Begin = 1; End = 0	0	

Discount Rate	13.01%
Growth Rate	0.00%
Net Present Value	$200,007.59

"As you can see there is an uneven cash flow projection for the next five years. If we discount these dollars individually we get:

$$\$20,000.00 / (1 + .1301)^1 = \$17,697.55$$
$$\$50,000.00 / (1 + .1301)^2 = \$39,150.40$$
$$\$80,000.00 / (1 + .1301)^3 = \$55,429.30$$
$$\$90,000.00 / (1 + .1301)^4 = \$55,179.15$$
$$\$60,000.00 / (1 + .1301)^5 = \$32,551.19$$

"The sum total is the "Net Present Value' amount shown on the bottom left of $200,007.59.

Figure 2-5 (continued)
(Right side of excel worksheet)

'alue of Money
3A - All Rights Reserved
lstars.com

Date

H	Year	Specific Cash Flows Discounted			
		Cash Flows			Total FV
	0	$	-	$	-
	1	$ 20,000.00		$	20,000.00
	2	$ 50,000.00		$	50,000.00
	3	$ 80,000.00		$	80,000.00
	4	$ 90,000.00		$	90,000.00
	5	$ 60,000.00		$	60,000.00
	6			$	-
	7			$	-
	8			$	-
	9			$	-
	10			$	-
	11			$	-

"Our simple formula of FV / $(1 + r)^t$ = PV continues to work in almost all of these problems."

"It really seems so easy," Hannah noted.

"That's right. Why don't we go ahead and see the last one. What is his name?" Nobel asked.

"That would be Nick Wang," John checked his clipboard.

"Go get him," Peter instructed.

In a few minutes Nick was standing before the group ready to present. Just as all the others, he was dressed very professionally. He was a little younger than the average, but demonstrated broad confidence and a big smile.

Introductions were followed by Nick launching into his proposal. He started out by saying he had always been a fan of Blue Chip Corporations and their potential for safety and returns. Then he pointed out that a well-crafted portfolio of moderate growth stock that payed dividends could be an excellent vehicle. If $200,000 were invested, a very nice return could be realized.

"Do you have any numbers you could share?" Peter asked.

Nick indicated he had personally selected five stocks for his pool and projected the collective dividends. Next year's total dividends received would be $8,485.00 and that would be followed by growth of 20%, 20%, 15% and 12% before leveling off with a continuing constant growth of 6%.

"What does that look like in terms of dividends?"

"That would be $8,485.00; $10,182.00; $12,218.40; $14,051.16; and 15,737.30 for the first five year respectively and then $16,681.54 in the sixth year."

"Do we liquidate after five years?" Peter asked.

"No, I suggest we continue holding the group indefinitely. I don't believe in churning when you have wonderful companies."

"Let me get this straight. There is no five year horizon," Peter clarified and continued questioning.

"There will be a horizon value in the fifth year, but that represents the sum total of all future dividends. It could be a sales price at that time, but I don't recommend it."

"What horizon value do you come up with?"

"Based on the $16,681.54 dividend in the sixth year I calculate a horizon value of $278,025.62 at the end of the fifth year."

"What overall return do you calculate for this investment?"

"I would think it generates a 12% annual return. Using the continuing value calculation for a constant growth stock I calculate:

$$HV = CF / (r - g)$$
or
$$\$278{,}025.62 = \$16{,}681.54 / (.12 - .06)$$

"That is the way I would have done it. So at a discount rate of 12% you get a net present value of $200,000, the original investment."

"That is right."

"Well, I can't fault your logic and you seem to exceed the overall return for the stock market over the last several years," Peter concluded.

Nick thanked the group for the opportunity to present and was excused.

"There you have it. They have all presented," Peter said.

"What a minute. I want to know about this last calculation. All of the other calculations ended after five years and this one continued on indefinitely. Is that why we had to calculate a horizon value?" Hannah asked.

"You got it. We could project dividends out for any years after we reach a constant growth situation and it wouldn't change the overall net present value. Our final result would be the same. The horizon value would change based on the final year of our projection, but once it is brought back to the present the conclusion is identical."

"You mean we have to bring the horizon value back to the present. I thought it was a present value."

"It is only a present value as of the date it was calculated. If that is the fifth year, then it must be brought

91

back for those five years." Nobel entered the data into his spreadsheet model:

Figure 2-6
(Left side of excel worksheet)

		TVM = Time V
		Copyright © 20013 ACB
		BusinessAll

Name[   ]

Standard Four Function Calculator		
S	Inputs	Results
Rate - Interest Rate		
Nper - Number of Periods		
FV - Future Value		
x PV - Present Value		$0.00
Pmt - Annuity Payment	$ -	
Type - Begin = 1; End = 0	0	

Discount Rate	12.00%
Growth Rate	6.00%
Net Present Value	$200,008.47

"See that the $278,025.62 is a value in the fifth year. When added to the fifth year dividend the total cash we receive in that year is $293,762.92. We can apply the same formula of $FV / (1 + r)^t = PV$ to each of the cash flows and then sum them up to get a total $200,008.47. Do you want me to go through the calculations?"

"No, I think I understand. So there are two important formulas, the present value of a future amount and the horizon value of a future stream of constant growth amounts."

"That's right. I think I have a financial wizard in the making."

Figure 2-6 (continued)
(Right side of excel worksheet)

alue of Money
A - All Rights Reserved
lstars.com

Date

H	Year	Cash Flows	Horizon Value	Total FV
x	0	$	$ -	$ -
	1	$ 8,485.00	$ -	$ 8,485.00
	2	$ 10,182.00	$ -	$ 10,182.00
	3	$ 12,218.40	$ -	$ 12,218.40
	4	$ 14,051.16	$ -	$ 14,051.16
	5	$ 15,737.30	$ 278,025.62	$ 293,762.92
	6	$ 16,681.54	$ -	
	7		$ -	
	8		$ -	
	9		$ -	
	10		$ -	
	11			

Specific Cash Flows Discounted

Suddenly, over the intercom came detective Hammersmith's voice. "What is our next move?"

"If you will continue to wait there, I will expose the murder shortly," Nobel said. Then turning to Peter he added. "Would you invite them all to come back into the conference room?"

Murderer Exposed

The tension was beginning to build for Hannah who had to get up from her chair and slowly pace in the space behind Nobel and Peter and in front of the window that overlooked the city. As John led the four contenders through the doorway at the far end of the room, Hannah stopped just short of the doorway and leaned against the wall.

The four entered the room and walked single file until they were standing behind the chairs on the other side of the table from Nobel and Peter. They stood there, waiting until they were asked to be seated, but that invitation never came.

"I'd like to apologize for putting you all through this exercise, but it was for a good purpose. I'd like to turn the time over to Nobel Merchant, who has something to say," Peter said.

"Your presentations were all excellent and gave me just the information I needed. You see, I've been hired by the homicide department to assist in the investigation of the murder of Halley Strong. She did not commit suicide as many have thought, but was intentionally murdered by one of you."

"The clue that she herself left just before she died and your presentations here have given me all the information I need to exactly pinpoint the culprit." Nobel then placed the picture on the table in front of them of the scrawled letter B in the trail of salt.

"I think Halley did not draw the initials of the murderer, fearful that the murder might come back before she was discovered and remove the evidence. The letter B had no significance for the murderer, but it gave an expert in finance all the information they would need."

"You see it is indeed the letter B, but not in the traditional sense. It is rather the Greek letter B for 'Beta.' Now beta has many uses in mathematics and particularly in finance, but more specifically it is used in the capital asset pricing model to represent risk. Average risk has a beta of 1.00 and anything higher is more risky. The beta she drew was not a small letter, but a relatively large and cumbersome letter. It was easy then to conclude that the murderer was a person who pursued high risk."

As Nobel was making his explanation, the group of four began to look nervously at each other. "From your presentations one of you demonstrated excessive risk as reflected by the very high rate of return on your project. It is so easy to conclude that with a return of 50% the murderer is indeed Lara Pullman."

Lara, realizing that she had been exposed quickly turned and pushed her way past the others and made a mad dash for the door. The others were all stunned; they didn't know what to do. Just as she reached the door, Hannah came from the other side of the room with a perfect hockey check and Lara went crashing to the floor. Lara lay in shock at the abrupt block as Detective Hammersmith and Sergeant Rice came through the door.

"Well done Merchant, well done," the detective repeated.

Nobel looked over at Hannah and gave a quick wink. "Well done Watson, well done."

Later that Evening

Nobel and Hannah sat on the porch swing reflecting on the events of the day. "You know I really had no idea where you were going with this," Hannah admitted.

"I would love to say that I had it all nailed down from the start, but in a way it was a very risky gamble. If she wouldn't have bolted, she could have denied everything and we might just as easily have been back to square one."

"Through the whole process I learned a great deal about finance and the time value of money. I can see where it has a lot of application to corporations and things like that, but I'm not sure how you would use it on a more personal basis."

"I have a couple of other models that might be of some help." Nobel went on to show Hannah a 'Loan' and a 'Life' model and explained their applications.

As the night was beginning to spread out across the neighborhood, Hannah wandered back to her home to reflect on her new career.

Summary of Concepts

Solving for Future Value Formula
$$FV = PV \times (1 + r)^t$$

Solving for Present Value Formula
$$FV / (1 + r)^t = PV$$

Solving for Horizon Value Formula
$$HV = CF / (r - g)$$

Where:
FV = Future Value
PV = Present Value
r = rate of return or interest rate
t = time period
HV = Horizon Value
CF = Cash Flow
g = growth rate

DIAMONDS

Learning Objectives

An understanding of:
Time Value of Money
Loan payment schedule
Lifetime financial plan

Spreadsheet Tools found at
www.businessallstars.com/calculator

Assessment found at
www.businessallstars.com/assessment

The Proposal

It was the morning after the day that Nobel
Merchant had solved a case for the local police
department involving the murder Halley Strong. He went
to his kitchen and glancing out the window saw his
neighbor, Hannah Watson sitting on the deck of her home
across from a handsome fellow. He was about thirty-five
years of age with a full head of black wavy hair. He could
have walked out of the pages of a fashion magazine.

They were in serious conversation when suddenly
the man pulled out a small box from his pocket and fell to
one knee. It looked for all intense and purposes that he
was in the act of proposing marriage. He extended the
small box toward Hannah with his left hand and opened it
with his right. Hannah appeared to be frozen in an
attitude of wonderment for a long minute and then looked
from the box to the man.

The couple rose to their feet and embraced. Nobel
looked away and didn't want to continue invading the
privacy of their special moment. He had breakfast and
busied himself working on a couple of research projects
at his computer.

It must have been around ten o'clock when there
was a knock at the back door. Before Nobel could leave
his work, Hannah came in and peeked her head around
the corner of the door frame. She was holding onto the
frame with her left and as Nobel looked up instantly
noticed there was no ring on her finger.

"What are you up to boss," she asked quite
innocently.

"I'm just trying to discover a new method for
projecting the moves in the market based on hedge-fund
activity."

"Oh," she responded.

99

"I noticed you had a visitor," Nobel offered.

"Yes, I did. It was Mario Horsley. He is a model I became acquainted with. We have been somewhat romantically involved for the last several years."

"Oh, I don't mean to pry," he said with every intention of doing just that.

"He has been out of the country on a shoot for the last month and just got back in town. I guess absence does make the heart grow fonder because…well…he just proposed to me."

"Congratulations."

"I didn't tell him yes, but then again, I didn't tell him no. He presented an absolutely incredible ring with several diamonds and one enormous stone in the middle."

"Are diamonds a girl's best friend?"

"I don't know."

"What is the hold up?"

"I've been thinking a lot about you and me."

This came as a shock to Nobel who had some feelings for Hannah and although there was great personal chemistry, he had never expressed anything more than friendship to her. "I'm not sure I understand."

"You see, these last few days have been really exciting to me. I love learning about all these financial models. I guess you could say I love modeling."

"Cleaver," Nobel noted.

"Anyway, I know there is nothing between us other than being neighbors and solving problems. But, I like what we have going and don't know if marriage right now is the best thing. Besides I just took Mario to the woodshed, so to speak."

"What do you mean?"

"He is basically pretty irresponsible. The ring he just showed me cost over $10,000 and when I asked him how he was going to pay for it, all he said was over time.

I demanded to know what that meant, but he was pretty clueless. You see modeling is a pretty random business and there are good times and bad."

"Did he have any details about the transaction?"

"He said it was a two year contract with a 5% interest rate."

"Did he pay anything down?"

"I don't think so. I pulled up your TVM model on my computer and showed him what the monthly payment would be:

Figure 3-1
(Left side of excel worksheet)

TVM = Time V
Copyright © 20013 ACB
BusinessAll

Name	Marlo's diamond ring

Standard Four Function Calculator		
S	Inputs	Results
Rate - Interest Rate	0.42%	
Nper - Number of Periods	24	
FV - Future Value	$ -	
PV - Present Value	$ 10,000.00	
x Pmt - Annuity Payment		($438.71)
Type - Begin = 1; End = 0	0	

Discount Rate	
Growth Rate	
Net Present Value	$0.00

"I divided the annual rate of 5% by 12 to get a monthly rate of .42% and entered 24 periods. I put in a present value of $10,000 and solved for the payment. It said he would need to pay $438.71 every month. When I asked if he had heard of a number anything like that, he was a little lost."

"It doesn't sound good."

"Then I pulled up the LOAN model you showed me last night and entered the loan amount, number of periods and the monthly rate:

Figure 3-2

	LOAN - Loan Amortization Schedule (up to 36 periods)				
	Copyright © 2013 ACBA - All Rights Reserved				
	BusinessAllstars.com				
Loan amt	$ 10,000.00				
Nper	24				
Rate	0.42%	Enter the annual rate / the number of periods per year			
Year	Beginning Balance	Total Payment	Interest Paid	Principal Paid	Ending Balance
1	$ 10,000.00	$ 438.71	$ 41.67	$ 397.05	$ 9,602.95
2	$ 9,602.95	$ 438.71	$ 40.01	$ 398.70	$ 9,204.25
3	$ 9,204.25	$ 438.71	$ 38.35	$ 400.36	$ 8,803.89
4	$ 8,803.89	$ 438.71	$ 36.68	$ 402.03	$ 8,401.86
5	$ 8,401.86	$ 438.71	$ 35.01	$ 403.71	$ 7,998.15
6	$ 7,998.15	$ 438.71	$ 33.33	$ 405.39	$ 7,592.76
7	$ 7,592.76	$ 438.71	$ 31.64	$ 407.08	$ 7,185.69
8	$ 7,185.69	$ 438.71	$ 29.94	$ 408.77	$ 6,776.91
9	$ 6,776.91	$ 438.71	$ 28.24	$ 410.48	$ 6,366.44
10	$ 6,366.44	$ 438.71	$ 26.53	$ 412.19	$ 5,954.25
11	$ 5,954.25	$ 438.71	$ 24.81	$ 413.90	$ 5,540.34
12	$ 5,540.34	$ 438.71	$ 23.08	$ 415.63	$ 5,124.71
13	$ 5,124.71	$ 438.71	$ 21.35	$ 417.36	$ 4,707.35
14	$ 4,707.35	$ 438.71	$ 19.61	$ 419.10	$ 4,288.25
15	$ 4,288.25	$ 438.71	$ 17.87	$ 420.85	$ 3,867.41
16	$ 3,867.41	$ 438.71	$ 16.11	$ 422.60	$ 3,444.81
17	$ 3,444.81	$ 438.71	$ 14.35	$ 424.36	$ 3,020.45
18	$ 3,020.45	$ 438.71	$ 12.59	$ 426.13	$ 2,594.32
19	$ 2,594.32	$ 438.71	$ 10.81	$ 427.90	$ 2,166.41
20	$ 2,166.41	$ 438.71	$ 9.03	$ 429.69	$ 1,736.73
21	$ 1,736.73	$ 438.71	$ 7.24	$ 431.48	$ 1,305.25
22	$ 1,305.25	$ 438.71	$ 5.44	$ 433.28	$ 871.97
23	$ 871.97	$ 438.71	$ 3.63	$ 435.08	$ 436.89
24	$ 436.89	$ 438.71	$ 1.82	$ 436.89	$ (0.00)

"I showed him how he was going to pay $438.71 every month for twenty-four months and the balance would slowly reduce each month."

"What did he think of that?"

"That is the problem, the more I showed him and became excited about the analysis the more he seemed to drift. You know I might just have taken that ring if he hadn't show so much disinterest. He was trying to give me a ring with priceless gems and I was sharing some planning models with what I think are priceless gems."

"You said one time that friendship is sacrifice, asking, listening and encouraging. He was not displaying any of those characteristics at the very point when he wanted me to commit my life to him and be not only his companion but his closest friend. I really had to step back."

"Did that pretty much end the deal?"

"Oh no, I wasn't through with him by a long shot. I figured that since I had a little of his attention, I was going for the whole enchilada."

"What do you mean?"

"There was that other model you showed me about how one could plan for retirement. I think you called it the LIFE model. I said 'Mario if we are going to be talking about a lifetime together, perhaps we should really start taking about a lifetime together.' I told him we were going to talk about a life plan and began asking the key questions: He is 35 years old right now and at what age does he think he will retire? He said about 65, he thought. I estimated that he would probably die at age 85."

"I'll bet he started to get a little nervous."

"He sure did. I knew he wouldn't know the answer to the next questions so I filled in the blanks for him. I estimated the real return on investment during his career would be about 9% annually, assuming he is wise with his investments. I next assumed the real return on investments during his retirement years to be about 3%."

"I asked him how much he wanted to receive each month from a plan when he retired. He threw out some ridiculous number and so I estimated that in today's dollars that would be about $5,000 each month. I assumed that he had zero in the bank right now that was committed toward retirement and that he would leave nothing when he died."

"I'll bet this long-range planning really freaked him out."

"Oh he was stunned. I entered it all in the model and showed him the results:

Figure 3-3
(Left side of excel worksheet)

LIFE® = Longterm Invest

Copyright © 2013 AC

Business

Name	Marlo Horsley's lifeplan

	Inputs
Current Age	35
Retirement Age	65
Death Age	85
Career Investment Real Return	9%
Retirement Investment Real Return	3%
Monthly Draw today	$ 5,000.00
Present Cash in the Bank	$ -
Cash left at time of Death	$ -

"He asked what it all meant and I said that he would need to start saving about $492.45 each month now for retirement in addition to paying $438.71 toward the installment loan on the ring. That was almost $1,000 per month beyond his living expenses, taxes, and everything else. I don't think he realized what kind of financial commitment he was asking when he asked me to marry him. I don't want someone who will take care of me, but rather an equal partner."

"Do you know how all those numbers are calculated and what they mean?"

"I think so. They all come back to that basic formula that you first showed to me."

Figure 3-3 (continued)
(Right side of excel worksheet)

CBA - All Rights Reserved
Allstars.com

ment and Financial Estimates

Date [   ]

	Outputs
Career Months	360
Retirement Months	240
Net Monthly Career Real Inv Rate	0.75%
Net Montly Retirement Real Inv Rate	0.25%
Cash needed in Bank at Retirement $	901,554.57
Career Monthly Investment Begin. $	492.45

"Do you mean:

$$FV = PV \times (1 + r)^t$$

"That's right. If you enter .25% real rate of interest per month, 240 months, zero future value, payments of $5,000 and solve for present value you get the amount Mario would need in the bank when he retires at age 65:

Figure 3-4
(Left side of excel worksheet)

	TVM = Time Val
	Copyright © 20013 ACBA
	BusinessAllsta

Name [   ]

Standard Four Function Calculator		
S	Inputs	Results
Rate - Interest Rate	0.25%	
Nper - Number of Periods	240	
FV - Future Value	$ -	
x PV - Present Value		($901,554.57)
Pmt - Annuity Payment	$ 5,000.00	
Type - Begin = 1; End = 0	0	

Discount Rate	
Growth Rate	
Net Present Value	$0.00

"Then if you clear the TVM model and enter .75% real rate of interest per month, 360 months, zero present value, future value of $901,554.57 and solve for

106

the payment to be paid each month during his working career you will get:

Figure 3-5
(Left side of excel worksheet)

TVM = Time V

Copyright © 20013 ACB
BusinessAll

Name

Standard Four Function Calculator		
S	Inputs	Results
Rate - Interest Rate	0.75%	
Nper - Number of Periods	360	
FV - Future Value	$ 901,554.57	
PV - Present Value	$ -	
x Pmt - Annuity Payment	$ -	($492.45)
Type - Begin = 1; End = 0	0	

Discount Rate	
Growth Rate	
Net Present Value	$0.00

"It really works out quite simply," Hannah said with confidence.

"You are really beginning to become a regular financial wizard. My only concern is that you sent poor Mario away with his tail between his legs."

"That's okay. I have great affection for him and quite possibly could marry him someday, but he really needs to think everything through and be serious."

MARKET

Learning Objectives

An understanding of:
Weighted Average Cost of Capital
(Small Company)
New Operating Capital
Invested Capital
Financing Capital
Family, Friends, and Fools
Angel Equity
VC (Venture Capital) Equity
R/E Retained Earnings Equity

Spreadsheet Tools found at
www.businessallstars.com/calculator

Assessment found at
www.businessallstars.com/assessment

The Neighbor

The supermarket was not very crowded that morning as Nobel worked his way up and down the aisles looking for the specific products he wanted. It was Monday morning and the time when Nobel liked to do his shopping. As he turned a corner he almost ran right over Lucille Goodman, his neighbor two houses down and across the street.

"Oh, excuse me," Nobel offered.

Lucille was a woman in her early sixties, who had let the gray in her hair naturally compliment her auburn locks. She had lived alone for several years after the passing of her Charlie. Never close neighbors, Nobel and Lucille had an occasional "Hello and a wave" type relationship.

"You'd better watch what you're doing with that run-away cart," Lucille instructed.

"I guess I wasn't paying attention."

Lucille nodded and moved on. She seemed a little cool and distant, but Nobel chalked that up to her annoyance at his almost running her down. He didn't think much more about it as he finished his shopping.

Later that afternoon, as Nobel was returning from an appointment he noticed Hannah, his next-door neighbor sitting on her porch. He raised one hand in acknowledgement and she motioned back a hand gesture that indicated she wanted him to come over. He parked in the drive and made his way there.

"What's up," He asked.

"I'm concerned about Lucille."

"Really," Nobel seemed a little surprised.

"Yes. I was talking with her yesterday and found out that her nephew was recently killed in a most bizarre accident."

"When did that happen?"

"Last week."

"Perhaps that explains her demeanor when I met her at the store this morning."

"Well, I think she needs our help."

Nobel's mind quickly moved to comfort, sympathy, and perhaps a food offering. "What do you think we ought to do?"

"We need to find out who did this dastardly thing."

"Wait a minute; I hope you aren't talking about another murder investigation."

"That's exactly what I'm thinking and we can help her most by finding out who did it."

"I thought you said it was an accident."

"It was only an accident to the extent that it was staged to look that way. I've been reading about it in the paper and I looks really suspicious to me. Why don't we go down and talk to Lucille about it?"

Nobel reluctantly agreed and so they crossed the street and walked to Lucille's home. They knocked and she came to the door.

"Lucille, I've brought Nobel over so you can tell him what you told me yesterday."

"Come in," she responded with a weary look at Nobel. They found comfortable spots in a small sitting room "I don't know what more there is to say except that my nephew was found dead in his car at the bottom of a ravine. It was apparently a drunk driving accident at least that is what the police are concluding. There is only one problem; my nephew could not drink alcohol. You see, it made him so sick that he never touched the stuff."

"Nobel and I have solved a couple of recent murders and I think we can help you," Hannah offered.

Nobel's mind began to imagine all kinds of situation that Hannah could drag him into. He was not a private detective or even a consulting criminologist. He was simply a finance guy. He didn't see how his limited capabilities could be used in a case that went beyond his own set of talents. "I think what Hannah is saying, is that there could be a remote possibility that we could be of some assistance. That would totally depend on the nature of the situation," he said with a bit of an exasperated look at Hannah.

"Go ahead and tell Nobel about your nephew," Hannah instructed.

"My nephew, Charles Porter ran his own company that made industrial boxes. He grew the company from a small shop in his basement to what I think if a fairly large operation. These last few years have been hard on Charles and I think his company was having some financial difficulty."

"See Nobel, this is right up our alley," Hannah chided.

"Charles' parent died when he was twelve and my husband and I raised him for the next few years. He was always very industrious and a good boy. If there is anything you could do I would really appreciate it."

"Where is his company located?" Nobel asked.

"The main offices are about 30 miles away, although his manufacturing facility is much further."

"Do you have access to his records and such?" Hannah questioned.

"I do, not only was I on the board of directors, but I have complete access to everything, because Charles trusted me so much."

111

"If it was foul play, is there anyone you suspect?" Nobel asked.

"I have complete confidence in everyone inside the company. I just don't know who could have done this and am at a loss."

Nobel continued the questioning: "Is it possible for me...us to talk to someone at the company? Maybe we could talk with the chief financial officer."

"That could be easily arranged. Let me call him right now." Lucille rang up the individual directly. "Hello Candace, this is Lucille. I would like to send a couple of people over to talk to you about Charles' death. They may want to look at some financial records and such. Would that be alright?" After a short pause she turned to Nobel. "When do you want to go?"

"How about tomorrow morning," He offered as he turned to Hannah with a questioning look. She nodded approval.

"Would tomorrow at ten be okay? Thanks."

The Company

The next morning Nobel and Hannah found themselves seated across the desk from a middle-aged woman in a well-appointed office. Candace Button had a bachelor's degree in accounting and had risen through the ranks at the company since its inception over the past ten years.

After brief introductions Nobel began his inquiry: "Is there anything you can tell us about the untimely death of Charles Porter, your president."

"I know these past three years have been financially difficult for the company. Our bottom line has been more negative each year. I think it is primarily due to the fact that one of our major customers went out of business and another was pirated away by a competitor."

"You don't think Charles was suffering from depression that could have led to suicide do you?"

"Absolutely not, he had a very healthy and positive attitude."

"Who do you think might have had a reason to do Charles harm?" interjected Hannah.

"I just don't know."

"May I look at the last set of financial statements?" Nobel asked.

"Certainly," Candace responded as she reached for a binder in the cabinet behind her. She laid the binder on the desk in front of Nobel and opened it to a tabbed section. "These are the statements for the last fiscal year end as of March 31st."

As Nobel perused the statements he asked, "Do you know what your weighted average cost of capital is?"

Figure 4-1
(Left side of spreadsheet)

wacc® = weighted average cost o
Copyright © 2013 ACBA - .
BusinessAllsta

Name

Net Assets (3 - 5 yr average)			Financing Ca
Cash	$	5,005	Bank Loan
Acc/Rec	$	3,750	Credit Line
Inventory	$	1,772	Mortgage
Other CA	$	375	Other Debt
Acc/Pay	$	3,221	Total Debt
Net Oper Cap	$	7,681	
			FFF Equity
Equipment	$	25,225	Angel Equity
Buildings	$	14,500	VC Equity
Land	$	-	R/E Equity
Other LTAssets	$	3,225	Other Equity
Invested Cap	$	42,950	Total Equity
Total Invested Capital	$	50,631	Total Financing

Candace sat in a long pause and then said, "I don't know what you're referring to."

"What is the source of your long term financing and the cost of each source. For example your long term debts and who has provided equity financing. As a result of that what are your periodic obligations for either repayment or financial return on that financing."

Figure 4-1
(Right side of spreadsheet)

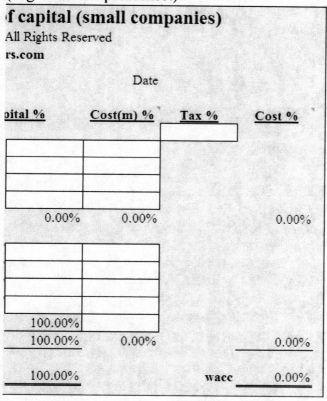

f capital (small companies)

All Rights Reserved
rs.com

Date

pital %	Cost(m) %	Tax %	Cost %
0.00%	0.00%		0.00%
100.00%			
100.00%	0.00%		0.00%
100.00%		wacc	0.00%

"I'm going to use a spreadsheet that I've developed that helps me focus on the weighted average cost of capital for a small company such as yours. On the left hand side I'm going to enter the total amount that needs to be financed. I call this the Invested Capital. The title asks for a three to five year average, but I'm going to enter your ending balances to get a feel for where you currently are. I'll enter the dollars in thousands. It looks like you are about a fifty million dollar company."

115

Figure 4-2
(Left side of spreadsheet)

wacc® = weighted average cost o

Copyright © 2013 ACBA - .

BusinessAllsta

Name

Net Assets (3 - 5 yr average)			Financing Ca
Cash	$	5,005	Bank Loan
Acc/Rec	$	3,750	Credit Line
Inventory	$	1,772	Mortgage
Other CA	$	375	Other Debt
Acc/Pay	$	3,221	Total Debt
Net Oper Cap	$	7,681	
			FFF Equity
Equipment	$	25,225	Angel Equity
Buildings	$	14,500	VC Equity
Land	$	-	R/E Equity
Other LTAssets	$	3,225	Other Equity
Invested Cap	$	42,950	Total Equity
Total Invested Capital	$	50,631	Total Financing

"Next I want to know your debt financing. Do you have any bank loans or lines of credit?"

"We have a bank loan for $10 million that carries an 8% interest rate. We also have a line of credit with the bank that varies, but at year end it had a balance of $5 million with an 8.5% interest rate."

"I'll enter an appropriate tax rate in the form. Then ten million represents about 20% of the fifty million in Total Invested Capital so I will enter it in the debt section along with its cost.

Figure 4-2
(Right side of spreadsheet)

All Rights Reserved

f capital (small companies)

rs.com

Date

pital %	Cost(m) %	Tax %	Cost %
		35.00%	
20.00%	8.00%		
10.00%	8.50%		
30.00%	8.17%		5.31%
70.00%			
70.00%	0.00%		0.00%
100.00%		**wacc**	1.59%

The five million in Credit Line is about 10% of the total and so I will enter that percentage along with its interest rate cost. The weighted average of these interest rates is 8.17% with an after tax cost of about 5.31%.

"Is there any other debt outstanding for the company that needs to be accounted for?"

"I don't think so."

"Has the company been able to meet its interest payments on time and any principle payments?

117

"We have a good relationship with the bank and have been current in every respect."

"Now we come to the equity financing sections. The first category is what is called FFF Equity and stands for Family, Friends and Fools. Is there any financing that has come from any of those areas?"

"Well Charles' aunt Lucille Goodman contributed $2 million when the company was started. Is that what you mean?"

"That is exactly what I mean. Were there any other friends of family that put up any financing capital?"

"I don't think so."

"Let's go to the next category. This is Angel Equity. Angel investors are affluent individuals or groups that put up start-up capital for young companies to get going. Was there any money from this source?"

"Not long after the company got off the ground there was an opportunity to secure a large customer, but we needed a major infusion of funds to purchase some equipment. Charles contacted a guy by the name of Paul Quickum. I don't know if you have heard of him, but he is a local multi-millionaire who made his money in real estate. He put up $20 million and took an equity position."

"A third category that I have listed is VC equity. That related to Venture Capital firms. These firms provide money to early-stage, high-potential, high risk, growth start-up companies. Have you ever been involved with these companies?"

"We explored that at one time, but they were so aggressive with us and demanded such a dominant equity position that we backed away. They wanted to own over 51% of the company and expected almost a 75% return per year. They were going to own us and then sell us off after three to five years. Charles just couldn't see going that route."

"That does raise the question of return. Do you know what kind of return Lucille expected from her investment?"

"She has never asked for any kind of annual dividend or anything other than a voice on the board of directors. I'm sure she expects that when the time comes to sell the company she will get her money back plus a share of the growth."

"What about the angel, Paul Quickum?

"Now that is another story. He has been good to work with except he does expect about a 25% return annually. When we were growing at about 20% per year, he was happy to see the value of his investment go up. We would pay him about 5% per year above the growth he could see in the company. Most recently, as the net income has been in the negative, it has been much harder to deal with him. I think he has been putting pressure on Charles to either sell the company or liquidate some of the underperforming assets."

"It looks like the rest of the financial funding has come either from Retained Earnings over time or from Charles original investment."

"That's right. Charles put up $2 million to begin with and then retained earnings have grown to $11 million. Retained Earnings were much higher three years ago, but with the negative earnings each of the last three years they have been reduced each and every year."

"When the company was doing well, what do you think Charles expectation for the company was?"

"I think he thought we could grow by about 20% per year."

Figure 4-3
(Left side of spreadsheet)

wacc® = weighted average cost o

Copyright © 2013 ACBA - .
BusinessAllsta

Name

Net Assets (3 - 5 yr average)			Financing Ca₁
Cash	$	5,005	Bank Loan
Acc/Rec	$	3,750	Credit Line
Inventory	$	1,772	Mortgage
Other CA	$	375	Other Debt
Acc/Pay	$	3,221	Total Debt
Net Oper Cap	$	7,681	
			FFF Equity
Equipment	$	25,225	Angel Equity
Buildings	$	14,500	VC Equity
Land	$	-	R/E Equity
Other LTAssets	$	3,225	Other Equity
Invested Cap	$	42,950	Total Equity
Total Invested Capital	$	50,631	Total Financing

"I'm going to enter that as the return expectation on both Retained Earnings and the Other Equity that Charles initially contributed.

"Lucille's $2 million financing is 4% of the $50 million, Paul's $20 million is 40%, Retained Earnings accumulation of $11 million is 22% and Charles initial funding is 4%, All told debt represents 30% of financing and equity represents the remaining 70%.

Figure 4-3
(Right side of spreadsheet)

f capital (small companies)

All Rights Reserved
rs.com

Date

pital %	Cost(m) %	Tax %	Cost %
		35.00%	
20.00%	8.00%		
10.00%	8.50%		
30.00%	8.17%		5.31%
4.00%	10.00%		
40.00%	25.00%		
0.00%	0.00%		
22.00%	20.00%		
4.00%	20.00%		
70.00%	22.29%		22.29%
100.00%		wacc	17.19%

"I'll enter the return expectations for each equity category as a cost to the company. I'll give Lucille a 10% expectation, Paul 25%, Retained Earnings and Charles 20%.

"The result is the weighted average equity cost is 22.29% and when that is weight averaged with debt the company total weighted average cost of all capital is about 17.19%.

"How does entering the tax rate effect the calculations?" Hannah asked.

121

"If you look at the Total Debt Cost it is 8.17%, but it is adjusted for the tax break that interest expense provides on the income statement. So the after tax cost of debt is shown as 5.31%. The Total Equity Cost is shown as 22.29%, but that number is carried forward to the Cost column unadjusted. There is not tax break for equity like there is for debt."

Hannah mused over the spreadsheet for a few minutes, trying to understand all the calculations. Then she asked, "Is all this going to help solve this mystery?"

"I don't know. I just needed to start somewhere and this seemed to be the best place," replied Nobel. Turning to Candace he asked: "So this is a complete list of all the financing?"

"It is for financing that has a cost. We have been pushing our Accounts Payable as hard as we can. If you look at the left side of your spreadsheet you will see that inventory is carried at a balance of $1,772,000. The corresponding Accounts Payable to the vendors of that inventory is $3,221,000. We have been delaying the payments on those payables just as long as we could to get the most out of our free financing."

"Has there been any backlash?"

"Not yet. They all realize the situation we are in and are trying to work with us. They really don't want to lose our business."

"There is one question I do have," Nobel said reflectively as he studies the spreadsheet. It shows here that you have over five million dollars in cash. That seems a little excessive for a company that is struggling to stay ahead of a declining bottom-line. I would think the pressure on cash flow has been significant."

"It's interesting you should mention that. We have struggled with cash flow until about January of this year, just before year end."

122

"What happened?"

"We suddenly have a major infusion of cash."

"Where did it come from?" Nobel asked.

Candace sat in silence for a moment and then said, "I don't know. Charles just showed up one day with $5 million in cash."

"How did you enter it in the accounts?"

"Of course it went into cash and the other side Charles just said to book it as a reduction in the Equipment account. He said we disposed of some old machinery and it was a recovery of book value. He didn't give me very much detail and I never was able to tie everything down."

"Didn't the auditors say anything?"

"Not really."

Nobel mused for a long moment. "Could I see any documentation that relates to the entry?"

"Sure, let me find it."

Nobel examined the bank deposit slip and any attached documentation, but it was all very clean. "I know it is a routine thing for auditors to send out confirmations on accounts receivable. Will you do something for me? I'd like you send out an inquiry to all customers, vendors, lenders, and investors asking telling them you are trying to confirm a cash deposit and see if any of them have any record of such an event coming from them on that date in that amount."

"I can do that."

Undisclosed

When Nobel and Hannah were back at his home he called his old friend at the police department, Detective Hammersmith. "I have a question for you. Who in the local metro-area is an underworld figure that would have the capability of extending a $5 million dollar cash advance?"

"Why do you ask?"

"I think there has been some foul play at work in the case of the death of Charles Porter and I suspect it relates to loan sharking that went bad."

"Well, there are the big guys and then there are the little guys. I don't think the big guys would ever get into a situation where a death would be the results. They are just too good. The little guys are more undisciplined. I can think of three individuals or groups that would fit your MO. One group deals primarily in illegal drugs, while another deals in prostitution and pornography and a third deals in a protection racket."

"I seriously feel that Charles Porter's company was in financial trouble, could not find the cash he needed to stay afloat and so resorted to the underworld. I suspect that he was unable to meet the demands of his lender and as a result paid the ultimate sacrifice."

"What makes you think so?"

"I know you will find this hard to believe but Charles did not drive off that cliff as the result of a drunk-driving accident. I know Lucille Goodman, his aunt has told you he never drank, but I believe her. The singular entry in his company books of an infusion of $5 million in January is just too coincidental."

"I'm beginning to think I should never doubt you. What can I do to help?"

"We need to ask the question, which of the three you just mentioned would Charles be most likely to do this unsavory business with? What contact or go-between set him up for this? Will you do something for me?"

"What is that?"

"Will you find out if there was any particular brand of alcohol that was found in Charles' car?"

"I have that someplace, but I'll get that for you."

"Thank you. Let me ruminate a bit on this whole thing and I'll get back to you." With that Nobel ended the conversation and turned to Hannah, "Did you get all that?"

"I sure did. Where do we go from here?"

"Why don't you go back and ask Lucille if she knew of any vulnerability that Charles had. While you are there, see if she will let you have access to his home where you can go through his personal things, including his papers, books, computer files and such. I don't know if he had a wife or anyone he was living with, but Lucille will be able to tell us. I'm going to see if I can do the same at the company."

Sometime later, Nobel and Hannah sat together and compared notes. "Did you find anything?" Nobel asked.

"I sure did."

"What is it?"

"Lucille didn't know of any particular issues that might have led me to any of the types of connections we are thinking about. Charles lived alone and she allowed me to go to his home and go through anything I wanted. While we were there she showed me where a key was to his filing cabinet. I went through all the papers and found a notebook with passwords for various programs on his computer. I then went through his computer from one end

125

to the other. Buried deep in one folder I struck pay dirt. It was a whole series of girls in the buff."

"You did better than I did. I found nothing and went through every file in his office. I couldn't get into some of his computer files and so who knows what I might have found there. But, from what you found, I think we can put together a connection between Charles and the low-level gang that deals in prostitution and pornography."

"I heard back from detective Hammersmith and he said there was a bottle of Spottswoode Sauvignon Blanc. This is quite a rare wine that is only sold at one place in the metro-area. He is going to check to see if the security cameras there show anyone purchasing a bottle on the day of the accident."

"I think we are really making progress. We may solve this thing for Lucille. I'm afraid she is not going to like everything we find."

"With any luck we will be able to connect the purchase of the wine to the murderer, who is part of the gang that deals in pornography and who advanced the $5 million to Charles. My feeling is that he was unable to repay the loan and its outrageous interest and so had to pay dearly. You would have to modify the spreadsheet and include the loan in the debt group. The only problem is to show the cost of that loan. How do you attach a cost that is represented by the life of an individual?"

Summary of Concepts

Weighted Average Cost of Capital (Small Company)
A calculation of a firm's cost of capital in which each category of capital is proportionately weighted. All capital sources - common stock, preferred stock, bonds and any other long-term debt - are included in a WACC calculation. All else equal, the WACC of a firm increases as the [risk] and rate of return on equity increases, as an increase in WACC notes a decrease in valuation and a higher risk.

The WACC equation is the cost of each capital component multiplied by its proportional weight and then summing:

$$WACC = \frac{E}{V} * Re + \frac{D}{V} * Rd * (1 - Tc)$$

Where:
Re = cost of equity
Rd = cost of debt
E = market value of the firm's equity
D = market value of the firm's debt
V = E + D
E/V = percentage of financing that is equity
D/V = percentage of financing that is debt
Tc = corporate tax rate

Businesses often discount cash flows at WACC to determine the Net Present Value (NPV) of a project.[1]

---

[1] http://www.investopedia.com/terms/w/wacc.asp

Net Operating Capital
This includes operating current assets minus operating current liabilities. Total current assets may include some items that are non-operating and need to be eliminated to arrive at operating current assets. Total current liabilities may include some current portion of long term debt that needs to be eliminated to arrive at operating current liabilities.

Invested Capital
This is the sum of the net operating capital and long-term operating assets. In some texts this is called the net operating assets or the total net operating assets. This is a misnomer because it confuses the operating function of the business with the investing function. Operating assets and liabilities are those that arise as the result of the revenue producing activities of the business and are clearly delineated in the statement of cash flows. Investing assets are similarly defined by the statement of cash flows. When operating current assets exceed operating current liabilities the residual is considered invested capital because of its required financing by interest bearing debt or equity.

Financing Capital
The compliment to invested capital on the left side of the balance sheet is the financing capital on the right side. It is the sum of all sources of financing that bears a cost. The weighted average cost of capital or WACC is the cost associated with these sources of financing. Financing capital is defined by the statement of cash flows and all related activities associated with it.

Family, Friends, and Fools

"In the early stages of a company, many entrepreneurs use 'friends and family' money. Your family will generally give you money because they have likely known you for most of your life, and you have somehow managed not to manifest career-criminal tendencies. If you've done well at school, have been able to hold down a job, and are perceived as being "reasonably intelligent" that's all a plus. This is basically the degree of "due diligence" that this friends/family group as investors will likely go through. Fools, on the other hand, haven't known you most of your life and have very little to go on to even know that you're not a career criminal (or possess those personality traits). So, what compels [them] to act so foolishly and invest in people [they] don't know that well, with ideas that are only half-baked? One, simple answer: A pathological desire to remain involved in the startup process.[2]"

Angel Equity

"An angel investor or angel (also known as a business angel or informal investor) is an affluent individual who provides capital for a business start-up, usually in exchange for convertible debt or ownership equity. A small but increasing number of angel investors organize themselves into angel groups or angel networks to share research and pool their investment capital, as well as to provide advice to their portfolio companies.[3]"

VC (Venture Capital) Equity

"Venture capital (VC) is financial capital provided to early-stage, high-potential, high risk, growth startup

---

[2] http://onstartups.com/tabid/3339/bid/216/Raising-Capital-Friends-Family-and-Fools.aspx
[3] http://www.entrepreneur.com/article/52742

companies. The venture capital fund makes money by owning equity in the companies it invests in. The typical venture capital investment occurs after the seed funding round as growth funding round (also referred to as Series A round) in the interest of generating a return through an eventual realization event, such as an IPO or trade sale of the company. Venture capital is a subset of private equity. Therefore, all venture capital is private equity, but not all private equity is venture capital.[4]"

R/E Retained Earnings Equity
A source of owner financing is retained earnings. In this case rather than paying out a dividend and then turning around and purchasing stock in the company, the owners decide to leave their earnings in the company for future growth. A lot of companies obtain external financing in this way. It increases the owner's claim on the business.

---

[4] http://www.privco.com/knowledge-bank/private-equity-and-venture-capital

CRUISING

Learning Objectives

An understanding of:
Dividend Yield
Dividend Discount Model
Capital Asset Pricing Model
Cost of Debt Plus Equity Premium Model
After-Tax Cost of Debt
Capital Structure Weights
Firm Specific Risk
Size Premium

Spreadsheet Tools found at
www.businessallstars.com/calculator

Assessment found at
www.businessallstars.com/assessment

Not Without Me

The interactions between Nobel and Hannah were becoming fairly regular. She would call him or come over each morning to find out what was happening. He enjoyed her attention, but wondered where this whole thing was going. She seemed to have it in her head that they were partners in a wonderful problem solving effort.

One morning he heard a knock at the back door and could hear Hannah open the door and call out, "Are you up and going?"

From the kitchen counter he responded, "I'm in the kitchen having breakfast."

"Great news, I just heard from detective Hammersmith that as a result of our efforts they have been able to nail down the Charles Porter case. It was murder and the gang members involved have been arrested."

"That certainly is welcome news. Have you talked with Lucille yet?"

"I'm going over in a few minutes. So what's up with you?"

"I was just reviewing a brochure from an executive training company who is sponsoring a cruise that I'm participating in."

"That's great, where and when?"

"The cruise will be next month, will start in Barcelona and end in Istanbul. I will be one of several presenters and they want me to talk about the weighted average cost of capital."

"Isn't that the model you used in the Porter case?"

"Not exactly, you see that was a model for a small privately held company. The more generic model for major corporations is a bit different. The intent of both models is to arrive at the same result, the cost of external funding to finance the business or the weighted average cost of capital."

"I need to hear this. I need to be there on the cruise," Hannah said with conviction. "If you couldn't tell already, I'm becoming quite excited about all this finance stuff. I want to learn. Is there any way I can come on the cruise?"

Nobel was taken aback. "I don't know…it is only four weeks out and I'm sure all the rooms have been sold."

"Do you have your own room?"

"Well, yes each of the presenters has a room to themselves."

"Then I'll bunk with you. Besides I'm your right hand man, Watson."

Nobel didn't quite know what to say. He did enjoy the synergy they seem to have together and he found working with her to be quite a pleasure. But, sleeping in the same room seemed to take the relationship to a whole new level.

She could sense his hesitation and fear of any intimate relations. "Listen, we are partners in a plutonic sense and nothing more. We are just doing this out of necessity. Besides, I want to learn all I can."

"I don't know if I can pull this off at this late date."

"You are one of the presenters, they'll make it work. I won't bother you with any of your official presenter stuff, I just want to be able to come and learn."

He reluctantly agreed, all the time wondering what he was getting himself into.

Barcelona

Nobel sat down at the little table reserved for speakers at the seminar. Before long he was joined by Sydney, a management consultant; Bill, an economist; and Frank, a marketing expert. After brief introductions Bill posed a question to the group, "How have you liked the cruise so far?"

"I really like Barcelona," Sydney offered. "I particularly enjoyed the Sagrada Familia by Gaudi and the interior pillars of the cathedral that emulated trees supporting the ceiling."

"When do you present?" Frank turned to Nobel.

"I'm scheduled for the morning of the two days at sea."

"What about you?" Frank looked toward Sydney.

"I'm up first thing in the afternoon."

"I'm doing the late morning," Frank offered. "I guess that leaves the late afternoon for you," he directed at Bill.

"That's right."

Turning to Nobel, Frank quarried, "Do you mind if I ask you a professional question?" Without waiting for a response he continued. "How do I calculate the return on my company stock? I see that is one of the topics you are presenting."

"Very simply it is the increase you receive from one year to the next," Nobel responded.

"That makes sense," Sydney said.

"I'm not sure I know what that means," Frank admitted.

"You referred to your company stock. How long have you owned it?" Nobel asked.

"I bought several shares at the beginning of July for $100 per share."

"Have you received any dividends?" Nobel pressed.

"They paid one just before I purchased the stock and I expect another at the one year anniversary, next June 30."

"How much will it be?"

"The last dividend was $2 per share and reports I've read say that next year's dividend should be ten percent higher."

"So the dividend you will receive as a reward for holding your stock for one year will be $2.20?"

"How did you get that number?"

"I multiplied $2.00 by one plus 10% which takes the original amount and adds the increase to get $2.20."

Last dividend times one plus increase
= next dividend
$2.00 x (1 + .10) = $2.20

"I guess that's right," Frank concluded.

"Do you think the company will continue to grow and pay an ever increasing dividend?"

"I would think so. They are a pretty good company with a long-term history of consistent performance."

"Is ten percent a good estimate of how dividends will grow for the next ten years?"

"Yea, I think so," Frank said confidently.

"Then the return on your stock will be its dividend yield plus the growth rate." Nobel stated.

"What is the dividend yield?"

"It is the end of the year dividend of $2.20 per share divided by the $100 per share price you paid at the beginning of the year," Nobel instructed. "The dividend yield for your stock is 2.2%. If we add that to the

135

expected growth rate in the price of the stock of 10% then the return on your stock is 12.2%. This formula is called the dividend-discount-model."

$$\underline{Next\ dividend\ divided\ by\ current\ price}$$
$$\underline{=dividend\ yield}$$
$$\$2.20\ /\ \$100 = 2.2\%$$

$$\underline{Dividend\ yield\ plus\ growth\ rate\ =\ return\ on\ stock}$$
$$2.2\% + 10\% = 12.2\%$$

"Interesting," Frank mulled.

Sydney turned to Bill. "What does the title e-comic mean?"

"I'm an economist with a comic twist. I assume that is why they invited me to speak. I make economics fun." Bill reported.

"Might we have a sample?" Frank asked.

"Sure, a fellow wandered down by a lonely beach where he found women's clothing laid out neatly on some towels. He looked out and saw four girl's heads bobbing above the water. He hollered, "Are you okay?"

They replied, "We are naked, how dare you come down here to spy on us!"

"Oh I didn't come to see you I came to check on the Great White Shark that was sighted."

The group all gave a polite chuckle.

"So it is with some countries and their economy, you can tell who is exposed when a crisis comes along," Bill said and then added: "Warren Buffett said 'You can tell who's been swimming naked when the tide goes out.'"

Monte Carlo

The next day the four speakers arrived at their designated table for dinner. "I so much enjoyed your assessment of Barcelona, how was your day in Monte Carlo?" Bill asked Sydney.

"It was wonderful. The tender into the port was a little choppy, but then Frank and I took a bus to the little village of Eze in the hills. The old buildings were really quaint and the winding paths ended up at the top with an incredible view of the whole coastline," Sydney responded.

Turning to Nobel, Frank asked, "I've been thinking about our conversation last night and wondered if your formula for finding the return on a stock works in every situation."

"It is one of the most reliable, but there are other methods for estimating the return on an investment in a stock. That one was an approach that is very company-specific based on dividend performance. There is another method that looks at how a stock compares to all other stocks in the market."

"How would you do that?" Sydney interjected.

"It is called the capital-asset-pricing-model or simply CAP-M and it looks at how volatile your stock has performed compared to all others," Nobel noted.

"What do you mean by volatile?" Frank pressed.

"Standard and Poor tracks the price of the five hundred largest companies in the United States that represents about 80% of total equity value[5]. We call it an index because it summarizes all five-hundred prices into a single number. The prices are always moving up or down and so the index goes up and down over time in a

---

[5] http://www.bogleheads.org/forum/viewtopic.php?t=55817

pattern like waves. We measure how high and low it goes, call this the normal movement of the market and give it a measure of 1.00. We then measure what the average return for the market is over time and find that it is some percent. Let's say if you invested in all the stocks in the index you receive an 11% return each year.[6]"

"So this model tracks the equity market generally, finds what it returns on average, and assigns a volatility measure of 1.00?" Frank reflected.

"That's right. Then we look at your company stock and see how much it rose or fell over time compared to the index. If the market went up 5% and your stock went up 10% or the market went down 5% and your stock went down 8% then it is more volatile and we would assign a measure greater than 1.00. Let's say for example it was twenty-five percent more active and so it might have a measure of 1.25."

"If it's movement was much less volatile and only went up or down half as much as the index then it might have a measure of .50. Volatility is a measure of risk. The more something is active, the less predictable it is and the less I can depend on a specific outcome. This volatility measure is called a company's beta."

"Does every company have a beta that measurers how volatile it is compared to the overall market?" Frank questioned.

"Most large companies do," Nobel clarified.

"I think I see where this is going. I can translate the beta to the expected return of 11% for the market and adjust my expectations of a return for my particular company up or down on that volatility measure."

"You've got it. We say that most investors would never invest in a company that paid less than what they

---

[6] http://pages.stern.nyu.edu/~adamodar/New_Home_Page/ datafile/histretSP.html

138

could get from investing in a really safe investment, like U.S. government bonds. So we establish a floor and say U.S. bonds have a beta of zero with no volatility. This results in a formula for the CAP-M where we add this volatility measure to the floor. If we expect a three percent floor and your company had a 1.20 beta then we would multiply the difference between the market return and the floor by the beta and add it to the floor."

"So it isn't multiplying 1.20 times the 11% market return, but by the 8% that the market-return exceeds the floor?" Frank noted.

"Now 1.20 times 8% is 9.6%. We add that to the floor of 3% and say that we would expect your company to pay a 12.6% return," Nobel summarized.

Beta times difference between the market return and the risk free rate plus the risk free rate
$$1.20 \times (.11 - .03) + .03 = .126 \text{ or } 12.6\%$$

"So which is it?" Bill questioned.

"What do you mean?" Nobel responded.

"Yesterday you said the dividend-discount-model resulted in one return for my stock and now you have a different return from the capital-asset-pricing-model. Which is it?"

"We can never tell exactly what the future will be and so we generally use both to cross check each other. I think yesterday's calculated return using the dividend-discount-model was 12.2% and today's return using the capital-asset-pricing-model was 12.6%. That is really pretty close and so we could expect a return in that neighborhood," Nobel explained.

Bill piped up: "That reminds me of the two old gentlemen talking. One asked, 'So how big is Monte Carlo?' The other replied, 'You can see the whole city from the mountain overlook.' 'Well, where I'm from it takes all day long just to drive around my city.' The other thought for a moment and then reported, 'You know, I had a car like that once myself.[7]' So it is with economics and returns on stocks, it all depends on your perspective."

Once again, the group at the table offered a complimentary chortle.

Those first few days Nobel had hardly seen Hannah. She busied herself with the other participants and put no demands on Nobel's time. When he arrived at his room each night after dinner she had already showered, was in her pajamas and in bed reading. "How was your day?" he asked.

"It was great, but I intend to stay out of your way and not interfere with any official business."

"These days at tourist destinations are free time and I wouldn't mind some companionship."

"Really," she offered innocently.

"Why certainly."

"Tomorrow is Rome. Do you have plans with anyone else?"

"Nothing definite, I hung out with a group of women executives in Barcelona and Monte Carlo and also at dinner, but if you have anything in mind I'll be glad to share it with you."

"Great, we'll wander Rome together."

"I know you must continue to dine with the other presenters and so I'll eat with these women."

"Sure, that's no problem."

---

[7] http://whyevolutionistrue.wordpress.com/2012/06/26/religious-diet-jokes/

Rome

The three men arrived at the table and sat down. They made small talk for several minutes and then Bill asked, "I wonder where Sydney is?"

"She went off by herself this morning, I hope she's okay." Frank seemed concerned.

Just then Sydney came walking into the dining room and took her place at the table.

"We were wondering about you," Nobel offered.

"Oh, I had the most incredible day," she seemed to glow.

"Was there anything in particular?" Bill asked.

"There were so many things, but I think the one that really did it for me was the Pantheon. I began the day thinking it would be my least favorite and it ended up at the top of the list. Isn't it like that? I just sat under that massive dome and could not soak it all in."

"Are you going to cover both the dividend-discount-model and the capital-asset-model when you present?" Frank asked Nobel.

"That and the cost-of-debt-plus-equity-premium-model or what I call C-DEP," Nobel responded.

"What is that?" Frank pressed.

"It is the third model that I utilized to nail down the return on equity."

"Is that all?" Bill asked.

"Yes, just the three," Nobel concluded.

"Okay, what is this one all about?" Sydney was now involved.

"I simply find the cost of the company's debt and mark it up by the amount that equity cost usually exceeds the cost of debt."

"We were talking about return on stock and now you're talking about cost of equity. What happened?" Frank queried.

"Common stock is a company's equity. What is cost for the company is the return for the stockholder. They are two sides of the same coin. So equity cost will be the same as return on common stock," Nobel explained.

"Are you suggesting that a company's common stock will always have a higher return or cost, as you say, than its debt?" Sydney asked.

"That is the general rule. I thought this conversation might come up today and so I did a little checking while I was out and found that Frank's company has five bond issues outstanding. They each have a different maturity ranging from five to twenty years. In addition, they each have a different coupon rate from 6% to 6.5%, but they are all rated "A" and have relatively similar yields-to-maturity in the 7% range."

"I think you lost me," Sydney admitted.

"Large investment grade companies obtain debt financing by issuing bonds to investors. These bonds are for a specified time period or maturity date and a definite interest rate, called the coupon rate."

"When the bonds are issued a rating agency will evaluate the company and determine how risky it is. They will look at its earnings record, how predictable those earnings are, what kind of financial reserves the company has and if there is any other debt outstanding. Then they will rate the company as either AAA, AA, A, BBB, BB, B, CCC, CC, C and so forth. Companies with the best rating of AAA will pay a lower interest rate because they are less risky. Those with more risk and a lower rating will have a higher interest rates. For each step down in their rating the possibility of default increases," Nobel pointed out.

"Why would anyone want the debt of a company that was going to default?" Frank asked.

"Some people are just willing to take that chance and receive a higher interest return. Once the bonds are issued an investor may decide to sell them in a secondary market to another investor. Over time the economy may change and interest rates may increase or fall for everyone. Even the company may change and improve its position or get worse in which case their rating may change."

"Bonds that were issued with an A rating and a 6.5% coupon rate may now be rated as BBB and need to pay an interested investor 7%. The price of the bond will change to reflect this and so the yield to maturity on the existing bond is what the current market expects. If Frank's company was going to issue new bonds today they would have to pay the higher rate."

"So how is equity more expensive than debt?" Frank asked.

"Equity or Stock is more risky than debt because interest on the debt is always paid before any dividends are declared for the stockholders. Also, if the company goes bankrupt then debt holders are paid first and stock holders only get what is left. Because of this higher risk, the market expects equity to pay a higher return. Equity premiums in the past have varied anywhere from 4% to 6%. If we add 5% to the yield-to-maturity of 7% then stocks should generate a 12% return. This is a specific risk return based on the company's individual yield on its debt."

Cost of debt plus equity premium = cost of equity
7% + 5% = 12%

"Let's see 12.2% from the dividend-discount-model, 12.6% from the capital-asset-pricing-model and now 12% from the cost-of-debt-plus-equity-premium-model[8]. That is a pretty tight range. Are they always that close?" Frank wanted to know.

"Heavens no, we are pretty lucky in this case. If a company has super growth then the dividend-discount-model could be significantly different. Other factors could also skew the other models."

"Well, Bill what do you have to offer?" Sydney asked.

"A bar tender in a Roman bar placed two drinks before a patron. The guy drank one and then the other. The bar tender shook his head and said, 'Each Saturday you have come in here and ordered three drinks, one for yourself and one for each of your two brother in another country. This time you only ordered two, is one of your brothers no longer with us?' The customer responded, 'No they are both fine, it's just that I've taken a vow of abstinence.[9]'" Bill said.

"What is the point?" Nobel queried.

"So it is with some countries and their economies, changing your ways and eliminating the overindulgence on debt spending is not so easy," Bill directed.

Polite but subdued laughter followed.

That evening when Nobel arrived at his room Hannah was watching the television. She turned to him and said, "I want to thank you for a wonderful day. The sites were amazing, but more than that it was so much fun. I don't think I have ever laughed so hard at some of your subtle humor."

---

[8] http://www.facebook.com/note.php?note_id=154212491386
[9] http://www.jokes.com/funny/walks+into+a+bar/walks-into-a-bar----beer-brothers

"It was my pleasure. Tomorrow we begin the presentations, take good notes."

A Day at Sea

"Are you all ready?" Frank asked Nobel as they sat at breakfast. "It's a big day today. I think I'm ready, but you never know. "What are you going to do as a follow-up at your next presentation?"

"I thought I'd talk about financing capital structure," Nobel explained.

"What do you mean?"

"When you go to buy a car you have to determine how much you will put down from your own equity and how much you are going to finance with debt. The percent of equity and debt out of the total cost of the car is the financing capital structure," Nobel said.

"Well, if what you say about equity being more expensive than debt, I would think I'd want to have almost 100% debt and no equity."

"Great answer, the only problem is that banks won't let you get away with that. They usually like you to have a skin in the game," Nobel clarified.

"In the corporate world the more debt you layer on to a company the worse your credit rating is and the higher the interest rate. There is usually some optimal ratio of equity and debt. One brilliant investor said that he liked to see a company with about 25% debt and 75% equity. The last thing in the world they want to do is issue new equity and this gives them the latitude to grow by issuing debt without endangering their bond rating."

"I think I'm getting it," Frank tried to visualize.

"Some software companies in the 1990s were so profitable they generated tremendous cash-flow and never needed to borrow any money. They were 100% equity driven. Then there are the capital intensive industries where they need a major expenditure in property, plant and equipment. They quite often carry a lot of debt. If we look at your company the cost of equity might possibly be around 12% to 13% and the cost of debt would be much lower."

"I think we calculated it to be around 7%," Frank offered.

"That is the market rate and what we used for a basis for the cost of equity, but the true cost of debt for a company is a little less than that," Nobel stated.

"What do you mean?"

"Interest payments are subtracted as an expense before we calculate what the taxes for a company will be. This means that taxes is reduced as a result of having interest expense. To get the true cost of debt for a company we have to adjust the 7% rate for the favorable tax impact. The other day I looked up what your company pays in federal and state taxes and it was around 40%. If I multiply 7% by the 40% I will get the tax savings, but I want the other part...the 60%, so I multiply 7% by 60% and find the real cost of debt as 4.2%."

Cost of debt time one minus the tax rate
$$7\% \times (1 - .40) = 4.2\%$$

"Boy that seems low. Are you sure that's right?" Frank wondered.

"I'm sure. If the company is 100% equity driven it will pay about 12.5% for financing. If it is 100% debt driven its credit rating will escalate way up to probably C and they will have to pay a real cost of debt of well above 15%. So there is some combination of equity and debt where the total cost is the lowest. But it is like I said. Some companies do not want to issue new equity so they might lower the debt level to give them room to maneuver."

Frank nodded as if he understood.

Venice

"I thought yesterday's sessions went really well. I had a lot of questions and interactions in mine. How about you Bill, did anybody get your spin?" Sydney led out.

"I think it went pretty well. I'm not sure how the combination of economics and humor is going over. I'll keep trying."

"Where did you go this morning in Venice?" Nobel inquired of Sydney. "It is always interesting to see what you find the most exciting about each of our stops."

"I loved the Rialto Bridge and all the little shops on each side of the arched walkway. I loved the architecture of the bridge and wonder why companies don't build commercial offerings as bridges over some of our highways and roads. It is kind of wasted space."

"I see that Frank has been drawn away by some of the participants and so I guess we won't have his company at the table this evening," Bill noted.

"Tomorrow is another day at sea and full of training sessions. Is everyone all prepared?" Sydney asked.

"I hope so," Nobel responded.

That evening Nobel and Hannah shared their enthusiasm for Venice. "I don't think I've ever had so much fun travelling."

"It is sad to say, but I agree. Have you been getting anything out of the training?"

"There is no question about it. I think I have found my true calling in life."

"Oh, what is that?"

"Finance!" Hannah said emphatically.

Athens

"It seems like we've all been so busy," Sydney notes.

"Well, a lot has happened in the last two days. It was a full day of trainings sessions, while we were at sea, and then today with the ship porting at Pyrenees and another full day in Athens. It has been busy," Bill agreed.

"What did you do today," Frank asked Sydney.

"I went to the Acropolis of course. I thought the Parthenon was everything I had hoped for. It is just too bad that so much of the decorative part was taken by the British and is in their Museum in London. I do think it is a worldwide tragedy that valuable historical items from so many locals are in museums in distant cities. I guess to the victors go the spoils. I still think it is terrible," Sydney stressed.

"I've got a question for you, Nobel," interjected Frank. "I went to your session yesterday and you introduced a format for calculating the weighted average cost of capital of WACC as you called it. I was just a little confused because you said that my company's cost of capital could be anywhere from 9% to 12%. Could you go over that once again for me?"

"I was going to go over a few things after dinner and so I brought my laptop. If you don't mind I'll pull it out and show Frank what I was talking about," Nobel replied. He reached down into his briefcase and extracted his computer. Placing it on the table between himself and Frank, fired it up and brought up the worksheet that Frank had been referring to. "This is a spreadsheet model that crunches the numbers (Figure 5-1)."

"That's the model I'm referring to," Frank said.

Figure 5-1
(Left side of spreadsheet)

WACC - Weighted ⍺

Copyright © 2013 A(

Business

Name	General Model

Input		**Input**
D/(D+E)	40.0%	Tax Rate
Cost of Debt	7.0%	Equity Premium
Dividend Yield	2.2%	Growth Rate
		Risk-free Rate
Beta	1.20	Market Return
Firm specific risk	0.0%	Size premium

"I enter various assumptions starting under the input title on the left side. The first is described as D/(D+E) and stands for the total debt as a percentage of the total external funding of debt plus equity. I looked up your company and found that it was about 40% funded by debt."

"Right below is the second input for the Cost of Debt and that is the 7% current yield-to-maturity we talked about the other day. Both the percentage of debt and the cost of debt correlate very closely with the A bond rating your company carries."

"The next input is for the Dividend Yield and is the result of the number we discussed before where we took next years expected divided of $2.20 over the current stock price of $100 and found a 2.2% dividend yield."

Figure 5-1 (continued)
(Right side of spreadsheet)

Average Cost of Capital

CBA - All Rights Reserved

Allstars.com

Date			WACC	9.0%

	Wght	**Output**	
40.0%		Debt% (KDAT)	4.2%
5.0%	33.3%	Equity % (KDEP)	12.0%
10.0%	33.3%	Equity % (DCFM)	12.2%
3.0%	33.4%	Equity % (CAPM)	12.6%
11.0%		Equity before adj	12.3%
0.0%		Cost of Equity	12.3%

"Next, going down the form is the Beta. Do you remember that we said your company is a little more volatile than the average stock in the market and carries a 1.20 beta?"

"I remember all that," Frank said.

As Nobel and Frank absorbed themselves in the spreadsheet Sydney and Bill were carrying on their own discussion and seemed perfectly happy to ignore the issue of WACC.

Nobel continued his explanation. "The next item is Firm Specific risk. Let's hold off discussing that input for a moment. Going to the next set of columns we need to enter the Tax Rate. Now, remember we said it was about 40% for both federal and state taxes?"

"I'm with you," Frank noted.

"The next item is the Equity Premium. We already talked about this one and we are going to use 5%

which is somewhere between the historic averages of 4% to 6%. Below that is the projected growth rate in dividends and you had offered a 10% rate. Do you see how each assumption is entered in its respective field?"

"I do," Frank nodded.

"The next two are for the Risk-free Rate and the Market Return. We talked about these also. The first represents the interest rate the U.S. government would pay on Treasury bonds and the second is the average return for all the stocks in the marketplace."

"We will ignore Size Premium for a moment. Now, we go to the next set of inputs and find that we need to enter the weights for how we will average the three estimations for return on equity. I have entered them all equally with 33.3% in the first two and 33.4% in the last."

"After all the inputs are entered the spreadsheet automatically calculates the WACC. In the last column we see that KDAT which stands for the cost of debt after taxes is 4.2%. That was calculated by multiplying the 7% cost of debt estimate from the first columns time one minus the 40% tax rate entry from the second set of columns."

"The KDEP represents the cost of debt plus the equity premium. It is simply adding the equity premium from the second set of columns of 5.0% to the cost of debt from the first set of columns of 7% to get 12%. This is the first of the three estimates of the cost of equity for the company."

"The DCFM stands for the Dividend Discount Model. Where companies don't pay a dividend then we use a calculation of total cash flow for the company instead. To call it DCFM is more generic than DDM. They should approximate the same thing. The form shows 12.2% which is the result of adding the 2.2%

dividend yield from the first set of inputs to the 10.0% growth rate from the second set of inputs. This is the second estimate of the cost of equity for the company."

"The last estimate of the cost of equity for the company is 12.6% and come from the CAPM. It is derived by multiplying the beta of 1.20 from the first set of columns times 8% which is the difference between the 11% market return and the 3% risk free rate from the second set of columns. We get 9.6% and add that to the floor or the risk free rate of 3% to get the 12.6%. This is the third and last estimate of the cost of equity."

"The spreadsheet multiplies each of the three costs of equity estimates by the weights and gets an average of 12.3% which is the cost of equity before any adjustments. So you see we have an after tax cost of debt of 4.2% and a cost of equity before any adjustments of 12.3%. We can't just add these two together and get the WACC because we have a little more equity 60% than debt 40%. So we multiply the 4.2% by the 40% and the 12.3% by the 60% and add the results together, which is 9.0%."

"This means that if the company continues with all these assumptions as we have entered them, then it will cost them 9% to obtain external funds to grow the assets of the company. Even if the company wanted to acquire another company and needed some external financing the cost would be 9% which is a combination of 40% debt and 60% equity."

"The program is kind of fun because you can change any of the inputs very quickly and see the impact on the WACC," Nobel seemed excited.

"What do you mean?"

"Let's drop the percent of debt from 40% to 20%, and with the improved bond rating the cost of debt from 7% to 5% and see what this does to the WACC."

153

Figure 5-2
(Left side of spreadsheet)

WACC-Weighted

Copyright © 2013

Fill in all cells ev

XL	Name	General Model		
Input				**Input**
D/(D+PS+CE)	20.0		%	Tax Rate
PS/(D+PS+CE)	0.0		%	Cost of Preferred
Cost of Debt	5.0		%	Equity Premium
Dividend Yield	2.2		%	Growth Rate
				Risk-free Rate
Beta	1.20			Market Return
Firm specific risk	0.0		%	Size premium

"Wait a minute," Frank said studying the screen closely (Figure 5-2). The WACC went up. How can that be? We just lowered our cost of debt," Frank complained.

"The average cost of equity also went down, but the percentage in the capital structure for debt went from 40% down to 20% and that meant that we added in more of the higher equity cost," Nobel explained.

"So lowering the amount of debt a company carries may not be beneficial to the overall cost of capital?" Frank theorized.

"Companies may want to be a AAA rated enterprise but they may be sacrificing a lower overall cost of capital for a higher one."

Figure 5-2 (continued)
(Right side of spreadsheet)

l Average Cost of Capital
ACBA - All Rights Reserved
en if the company has no debt

		Date		Calc. WACC	9.88	
		Weight		**Output**		
40.0	%			Debt % (KDAT)	3	%
0.0	%			Pref % (KPS)	0	%
5.0	%	33.33	%	Equity % (KDEP)	10	%
10.0	%	33.33	%	Equity % (DDM)	12.2	%
3.0	%	33.34	%	Equity % (CAPM)	12.6	%
11.0	%			Equity before adj	11.6	%
0.0	%			Cost of Equity	11.6	%

"On the other hand a company may make a conscience decision to have more debt and a lower credit rating."

"Are you two about ready to join the real world," Sydney asked.

Nobel and Frank looked away from the computer screen at the other two. "Sorry, we will put this away," Nobel responded as he closed down the computer and put it back in his bag.

"I was just about to have Bill tell us one of his profound stories that he shares with his sessions," Sydney added.

"We'd love to hear it," Frank encouraged.

"Well, I couldn't resist going up on top of Mars hill, right next to the Acropolis. It is where Paul stood when he preached in the Bible. I looked out over the city of white buildings and saw that the recent rain had made the paint run. So I called out in a loud voice, 'Repaint, repaint, and thin no more.[10]' The Greeks need to put more equity into their economy and not as much debt."

Everyone groaned just a little with their smile.

Later that evening Hannah was excitedly remarked to Noble: "This has been an incredibly rich and rewarding trip. The wonderful cities, and the fun we have had, but also the training sessions. I do have one question though."

"What is that?"

"In your session you said the capital structure where we look at the perce ntage of debt relative to the combined debt and equity was based on market values and not book values. What did you mean?"

"The amount of stockholder's equity that is shown on the balance sheet is a book value number and come from historic dollars that are either invested by the stockholders or retained by the company. If we divide that number by the number of shares outstanding we may get a something like $5 per share. The stock actually trading in the market may be selling for $20 per share. The $5 is a book value and the $20 is a market value."

"I think I get it."

"People who purchase stock in the market don't expect a return based on a book value number, but rather a return based on what they paid for the stock…a market value number."

"I'm going to have to think about this for a while."

---

[10] http://www.frtommylane.com/stories/jokes/repaint.htm

Istanbul

"It has been a great cruise," Bill offered.

"It really has," Frank added.

"I'm really going to miss the incredible cities we have been able to see," Sydney noted.

"Will you miss the presentations we made?" Nobel questioned.

"I've quite enjoyed the sessions," Bill said.

"Did anyone make the connection between your humor and economics?" Frank pressed.

"Oh, sure everything went over very well. I was a big hit. You know I've signed up to repeat for five more cruises. What about you?" Bill asked everyone.

The other three all nodded agreement, but did not offer the exact details of what they had committed to. "I can't wait to hear what the big attraction was in Istanbul," Bill looked at Sydney.

"You might think I would say Topkapi Palace, Blue Mosque, Hagia Sophia, or Underground Cisterns--- nope. For me it was the Grand Bazaar all the way. I love the marketplace, the energy, and the excitement. I could have spent my whole day there. You are always pressing me for what was interesting at each city; didn't anyone else have an experience worth discussing?" Sydney wanted to know.

"I had a very strange experience. I like to wander around and talk to the people. I was in the spice market and encountered an old fellow at one of the stands. We got to talking and when I told him I was a teacher and finance consultant who traveled the world he became very interested. He told me about an old book he had been given by his grandfather, called 'The Merchant.' He said he had no descendants, but felt it needed to be shared with the world. I was very interested, he hurried off and so I kept wandering the market," Nobel explained.

"After a while I was about to leave and he hurried up to me and thrust a small book into my hands. He said it was a gift and would know what to do with it."

"Did you keep it?" Frank asked.

Nobel reached into his bag, pulled out a small leather bound volume and laid it on the table.

"Do you mind?" Bill asked reaching for the book.

Nobel nodded his approval and Bill picked up the book. He examined it very reverently, turning the well-worn pages with great care. "It appears to be in a language, I'm not familiar with," Bill noted.

Everyone watched quietly and when Bill had completed his inspection each of the others in turn examined the work. Finally, Sydney handed it back to Nobel. "What are you going to do with it?" she asked.

"First I'm going to find someone who can translate it and then I'm going to try and make it available to as wide an audience as I can—depending on how I feel about its contents."

"Will you keep us informed about your progress?" Frank asked.

"Of course," Nobel affirmed.

"Do you have any last story for us?" Sydney looked at Bill.

Bill thought for a moment and then said, "A fellow went into a café in Istanbul and found a seat at a table. He happened to overhear a conversation between two men at the next table. One said that his wife made him go to a marriage counselor. When they got there she went on and on about how she felt no romance, no passion, received no affection and such. Finally, the counselor stood up walked around the desk, gathered up the wife in a huge embrace and gave her a passionate kiss on the lips. Then the counselor turned to the husband and said the wife needed that kind of treatment three times every week. The husband responded that he would be willing to bring her in on Mondays and Wednesdays but that he golfed on Fridays."

"So what is the moral to that story?" Frank asked.

"The Turkish economy is very delicate and while you have to give the people what they think they want, it almost certainly could get you into trouble."

"You are amazing," Nobel noted as the other two seemed amused.

Just then Bill reached up and placed his right hand on his chest and began breathing heavily. "Are you okay?" Sydney reached out with concern.

"I don't know."

Everyone drew closer as Sydney stood up and went around behind Bill. Others at a near-by tables looked on with alarm. Soon two of the servers were at the table. Bill stood up and seemed to want to leave. "I'll come with you," Sydney offered as the two of them left.

"I hope he is okay," Frank said as Sydney and Bill left the dining room. "How old do you think he is?"

"I would say in his mid-sixties. I know he is retired and looking forward to a life teaching seminars on cruise ships," Nobel replied.

"I'm sure he is in good hands. Sydney is young and seems very capable of handling any emergency," Frank observed.

The two of them sat in silence for a few minutes and then Frank asked, "Were you going to tell me about those last two lines on your WACC spreadsheet?"

"Sure, I'll be glad to. If you don't mind waiting a minute, I'll go get my computer and it will only take me a second," Nobel was up and away.

Figure 5-3
(Left side of spreadsheet)

WACC-Weighted

Copyright © 2013

Fill in all cells ev

XL Name	General Model		
Input			**Input**
D/(D+PS+CE)	40.0	% Tax Rate	
PS/(D+PS+CE)	0.0	% Cost of Preferred	
Cost of Debt	7.0	% Equity Premium	
Dividend Yield	2.2	% Growth Rate	
		Risk-free Rate	
Beta	1.20	Market Return	
Firm specific risk	3.0	% Size premium	

He returned carrying his laptop and placed in on the table between them. After turning it on and bringing up the spreadsheet he entered all the original data from the first case he had discussed with Frank from the previous day which reflected the 9.0% WACC for the XYZ Company. "Now, these last two lines across the bottom are for entering special situation percentages. The first one adds a factor for Specific Risk. It can be anything up to 6% and represents an adjustment to the WACC for things that make the company more risky."

"These risk factors could be a lot of things, but I have grouped them into six basic categories: (1) Key Customer dependency; (2) Key Personnel Dependency;

Figure 5-3 (continued)
(Right side of spreadsheet)

l Average Cost of Capital

ACBA - All Rights Reserved

en if the company has no debt

		Date		Calc.	WACC	12.04	
		Weight		**Output**			
40.0	%			Debt % (KDAT)	4.2		%
0.0	%			Pref % (KPS)	0		%
5.0	%	33.33	%	Equity % (KDEP)	12		%
10.0	%	33.33	%	Equity % (DDM)	12.2		%
3.0	%	33.34	%	Equity % (CAPM)	12.6		%
11.0	%			Equity before adj	12.267		%
2.0	%			Cost of Equity	17.267		%

(3) Key Supplier Dependency; (4) Potential Lawsuits; (5) Potential Regulatory Change; and (6) Potential New Competition," Nobel explained.

"It seems like the first three are dependency issues of one kind or another."

"That's right. When a company is too dependent on dominant customers, suppliers, or company people they are in a position when any change could be very detrimental. We need to adjust the WACC upward to compensate for this added risk."

"The last three are potential externalities that could make the continuation of past practices compromised," Nobel concluded.

"Our company is very dependent on the CEO who was the founder and the real genius behind most of our new products and market strength. If he were to leave, I don't know what we would do," Frank admitted.

"Let's add a 3% risk adjustment for that to our spreadsheet. The next item is for a Size Adjustment[11]."

"Very large corporations have no size adjustment, but companies that are smaller must add a factor for size. There is some debate as to what causes this adjustment, but there is little challenge about its existence. Our spreadsheet suggests that up to a 4% add on may be required because of size. Anything less than about two billion dollars in assets should have something added for size. When I looked at your company it was around 1 billion and so I've suggested adding about 2%."

"As you can see the effect (Figure 2-3) of these two adjustments the WACC could jump from 9% all the way up to 12%. That is a fairly realistic number for a smaller company with some specific risks."

"That is pretty amazing. So what you're saying is a company would have to expect to pay about 12% on average for external financing to support expansion of assets, acquisition of other companies, or whatever reason," Frank reiterated.

"Yes."

Sometime later that evening Nobel ran into Sydney who seemed very disturbed. "What is the matter?" He asked.

"It's Bill. We went down to the ship's medical center and the ship's doctor was there. He took Bill right in and worked on him. It was a massive heart attack. Bill died and there was nothing anyone could do."

"You've got to be kidding," Nobel exclaimed.

---

[11] http://ccrc.morningstar.com/PDF/Methodology/(Methodology)%20SBBI%20Valuation%20Essentials.pdf

"No I'm not. The last thing he said to me was that he was so happy. He was doing what he loved on a cruise ship to some of the most wonderful cities on earth and being attended to by me. That was so sweet and then he just was gone."

"I can't imagine someone dying on a cruise ship," Nobel protested.

"The doctor said it happens more often than you think."

Nobel was still reeling when he ran into Hannah. He reported what had happened and it seemed to put a damper on what was to be a wonderful ending to an exciting adventure.

"Maybe to take your mind off of sad things, I was sitting at the dinner table with my usual group and we were joined by a fellow who had some questions about your session. I was able to address most of them, but he was very concerned about the whole cost of debt thing. I told him I had an inside connection with the presenter and would see if you would consult with him. What do you think?"

"I don't really think I'm up to it right now."

"That's okay, he lives in Denver and I took his number. I told him we would call him and help out anyway we could."

Nobel gave Hannah a sideways look.

Summary of Concepts

Dividend Discount Model
The **dividend discount model** (DDM) is a way of valuing a company based on the theory that a stock is worth the discounted sum of all of its future dividend payments. In other words, it is used to value stocks based on the net present value of the future dividends. The equation most always used is called the **Gordon growth model**. It is named after Myron J. Gordon, who originally published it in 1959; although the theoretical underpin was provided by John Burr Williams in his 1938 text "The Theory of Investment Value."

Dividend Yield
The **dividend yield** or the **dividend-price ratio** of a share is the company's total annual dividend payments divided by its market capitalization, or the dividend per share, divided by the price per share. It is often expressed as a percentage.

Capital Asset Pricing Model
The **capital asset pricing model (CAPM)** is used to determine a theoretically appropriate required rate of return of an asset, if that asset is to be added to an already well-diversified portfolio, given that asset's non-diversifiable risk. The model takes into account the asset's sensitivity to non-diversifiable risk (also known as systematic risk or market risk), often represented by the quantity beta (β) in the financial industry, as well as the expected return of the market and the expected return of a theoretical risk-free asset.

Capital Structure

In finance, **capital structure** refers to the way a corporation finances its assets through some combination of equity, debt, or hybrid securities.

Cost of Debt plus Equity Premium

Bond yield plus risk premium method is used to calculate cost of common equity for a firm. This is not an exact rate but an estimate of the cost. Bond yield plus risk premium equals the cost of debt, in this case the bond yield plus the risk premium.

Cost of Equity

The **cost of equity** is the return (often expressed as a rate of return) a firm theoretically pays to its equity investors, i.e., shareholders, to compensate for the risk they undertake by investing their capital.

Expected Growth Rate

This is the expected constant growth for dividends into the future. Growth cannot exceed the cost of equity.

Firm Specific Risk

A category of unsystematic risk is referred to as "specific company risk." Historically, no published data has been available to quantify specific company risks. However as of late 2006, new research has been able to quantify, or isolate, this risk for publicly traded stocks through the use of Total Beta calculations. P. Butler and K. Pinkerton have outlined a procedure which sets the following two equations together:

Total Cost of Equity (TCOE) = risk-free rate + total beta*equity risk premium TCOE = risk-free rate + beta*equity risk premium + size premium + company-specific risk premium

The only unknown in the two equations is the company specific risk premium.

Size Premium
Investors who invest in small cap stocks, which are riskier than blue-chip stocks, require a greater return, called the "size premium." Size premium data is generally available from two sources: Morningstar's (formerly Ibbotson & Associates') Stocks, Bonds, Bills & Inflation and Duff & Phelps" Risk Premium Report.

Weighted Average Cost of Capital
The WACC is the minimum return that a company must earn on an existing asset base to satisfy its creditors, owners, and other providers of capital, or they will invest elsewhere.

DEBT

Learning Objectives

An understanding of:
Bonds
Rating of debt
Interest rate schedule

Spreadsheet Tools found at

www.businessallstars.com/calculator

Assessment found at

www.businessallstars.com/assessment

A Death in Denver

Nobel answered the phone and it was a person by the name of Cyril or rather Cy Chapman who said he had been talking with Hannah on the cruise and that she spoke very highly of what Nobel could do.

"What exactly did she say?" Nobel asked.

"She said you could solve murder mysteries."

Nobel rolled his eyes. "I think Hannah is exaggerating my capabilities."

"Well, it isn't exactly the murder of an individual but rather a company. The effect of which will put hundreds of people's careers at risk."

"When is this going to happen?"

"Any day now I expect the company to declare it will no longer be able to meet their obligations."

"I'll help in any way I can."

"Good, if you could fly to Denver at the earliest convenience I will cover all costs and pay handsomely for your time."

Later that day Nobel cut through the gate that separated their two yards and knocked on Hannah's back door. She was used to knocking and walking right in on Nobel, but he could not quite bring himself to do the same. In a moment she came to the door and ushered him in. She was on her phone at the time and seemed quite involved.

When she hung up she turned to Nobel. "It is Mario. He is concerned that I haven't called him back in a while and thinks that I may be spending too much time with you."

"I don't know what to say."

"It is okay. I'm going to have lunch with him tomorrow and will straighten everything out."

Nobel didn't know how to respond and so he just jumped right to the point. "I came over to say that Cy Chapman called me from Denver. He is the fellow you met on the cruise and wants me to consult with him. What do you know about all this?"

Hannah thought for a moment and then began: "He started a high-tech company about ten years ago. I can't remember what the product was, but they had a good market. They did pretty well for about five years and then growth began to overwhelm them. They needed cash and it appeared his only option was the venture capital market."

"They came in with a big infusion of cash, but also took a controlling interest in the company. After about a year they reorganized and cut Cy out. They brought in new management and then about two years ago they took the company public with an Initial Public Offering (IPO)."

"Cy tried to get back into the company, but didn't have the funds to acquire enough stock to regain control. About a year ago the company issued some bonds in the debt market."

"I suppose I should go and see him," Nobel responded.

"When are we going? Remember, I'm Watson."

"I told him I couldn't come until Monday."

"That works for my schedule."

Deception

Nobel and Hannah arrived at Cy's office and were greeted by his assistant. Soon they were ushered into meet Cy. It was a beautiful modern office in a corner of the 21st floor of the building.

"It is good to see you again," Hannah offered.

Cy recognizing both Hannah and Nobel responded. "I'm not sure what there is to be done at this point."

"What exactly do you mean?" Nobel asked.

Cy picked up a file folder from his desk and handed it to Nobel. "Here is the last set of financial statements. They just don't seem to make any sense."

"I'm not following," Nobel shot back.

"When I built the company and before the venture capital people came along, we prided ourselves on producing quality products that had real market impact. Some people thought we were too obsessed with quality and our bottom line was not strong enough. I suppose they were right. We had a very difficult time getting all the financing we needed in a high growth situation. A lot of the people we approached for funds were nervous about our profitability."

"As a last resort we had to go to the venture capitalists. They provided all the funding we needed to take the operation to the next level, but in return demanded a controlling financial interest in the company. At first I accepted their input, because they seemed supportive of our strategic direction."

"Then after a while they began to put pressure on us to cut expenses and boost the bottom-line. I tried to resist, but they had all the chips and prevailed in the end. I was ushered out of the company and they brought in their own people."

170

"Did it affect the quality of the product?" Hannah asked.

"Not at first. As time went on it most certainly did. Our customers complained, but remained loyal, I suppose because of the established market and limited competition. They virtually had no alternative. As I would visit with employees who still worked there, they reported all kinds of problems that seemed to be swept under the carpet."

"When the venture capitalists bailed and took the company public the due diligence that was performed didn't expose the vulnerability of the company?" Nobel asked.

"That's what I couldn't understand. It was almost as if the venture capital people, the lawyers and accountants were all reading from the same script. They all made money with the deal and so pushed it through. The price of the stock held up pretty well and then the company came out with its first bond issue. Once again I thought the rating agency and analysts would see how thin things were getting, but they gave the bonds an AA rating."

"Do you think that was too strong?" Nobel pressed.

"I don't think there is any question about it."

Hannah puzzled for a moment and then asked: "Tell me once again about these ratings."

"When a company wants to borrow a great deal of money, even more than a local bank can handle, they will go to an investment bank who will sell the company's bonds to the public and raise the cash needed. Bonds have a predetermined face value and maturity date, along with what is called a coupon rate. That is the interest rate to be paid on the bonds."

"A company might want to raise $100 million dollars to build a new plant. The investment bank would sell enough bonds to get their commission and net the company the $100 million. The bonds would have a life of say 20 years which means the company gets to use the whole $100 million for twenty years and then pay it all back at the end."

"It is different from a mortgage where the amount you borrowed is gradually paid back over the life of the loan. The company doesn't pay back any principle until the end. What they do pay is interest on the debt over the life of the bond. That interest is the coupon rate. Let us say that was five percent. The company would pay five percent of the $100 million every year or $5 million to all those people who owned those bonds."

"What is critical, when issuing bonds, is the rating an agency gives the company. It is like a credit rating for a person. The very best rating is AAA and results in the lowest coupon or interest rate. Next is AA, followed by A, and then BBB, BB, B, CCC and so forth. The lower the rating the higher the interest rate and the greater the potential the company may at some point go under and not be able to repay the loan," Nobel instructed.

"So you say the company received a double A rating?" Hannah reiterated.

"That's right, but it made no sense. Once again there had to be some collusion between all the money people," Cy said with exasperation.

"So you think the rating should have been lower with a higher interest rate?" Hannah pressed.

"No question."

"Where does the company stand today?" Nobel asked.

"My sources tell me if they make it another month they will be lucky."

"I suppose if investors knew how bad the company was, the stock price would tumble and the market rate on the bonds would escalate," Nobel noted.

"I thought you said the interest rate on the bonds was set at 5%," complained Hannah.

"It is set at that rate when the bonds are issued. When they trade in the secondary market where someone holding some of the bonds decides to sell them to someone else, the redeemable face amount of the bonds and the monthly interest payment don't change. Those are locked in by contract. But if the company is suddenly in trouble then their credit rating would change and the market rate of interest would go up. That is accounted for in the price the original owner will sell the bonds at."

Nobel pulled out his computer and brought up the TVM spreadsheet. "Do you remember the spreadsheet we used to look at time value of money problems?"

"Sure I do," Hannah responded.

"I will enter $100 as the future value the bonds will pay back, $5 as the annual interest payment and 18 as the years until maturity."

"If I enter an interest rate of 8% assuming the bonds are now more risky because the company is in trouble and click on PV to calculate the present value, I will see that someone would only be willing to pay $71.88 million for all those bonds today. They pay the lower amount and get $5 million every year as the interest payment and $100 at the end of eighteen years. The lower purchase price allows them to earn a real rate of eight percent on the investment."

"The poor people who initially bought the bonds for $100 million and sell them for $71.88 million just took a $28.12 million loss," Hannah figured.

Figure 6-1
(Left side of the TVM spreadsheet)

	Standard Four Function Calculator		
TVM = Time V			
Copyright © 20013 ACE			
BusinessAI			
Name			
S		Inputs	Results
	Rate - Interest Rate	8.00%	
	Nper - Number of Periods	18	
	FV - Future Value	$ 100.00	
x	PV - Present Value		($71.88)
	Pmt - Annuity Payment	$ 5.00	
	Type - Begin = 1; End = 0	0	

"Exactly right, that is what is potentially going to happen in this case with Cy's company assuming the market learns that things are really bad for the company."

"I guess the stock would suffer a similar fate."

"I've got a real dilemma. If I trade on the insider information that I've got, I could go to jail. The trouble is that I think the company is in real danger and a lot of people could get hurt," Cy concluded.

"You mean like the bond holders and the stockholders," Hannah offered.

"Not only investors but all the employees. They could lose their jobs and lively-hoods. They could also lose their pensions and retirement. This could hurt so many people in so many ways."

"But you don't know those things for sure," Hannah challenged.

"You're right, I don't." Turning to Nobel, Cy asked. "Do you have any way we could check the numbers?"

"I have a little spreadsheet that does some quick and dirty calculations like those that a normal rating agency would do. We could see what kind of rate the bonds could potentially be at."

"That would be great," Cy seemed pleased.

Nobel opened a spreadsheet, took the financials that Cy had given to him and began entering some data. What is the name of the company?"

"Garbenzoa-Tech."

Nobel entered that in the title row. "I'm going to enter the financial information from the last audited financial report that you just handed to me. The first four items come from the Income Statement: Sales or Revenue for the year, EBIT or the Earnings Before Interest and Taxes, Interest Expense, and Net Income."

"The next three items I get from the Statement of Cash Flows: Depreciation Expense, Cash Flows from Operations, and Capital Expenditures. The last three come from the Balance Sheet: Long-Term Debt, Total Debt, and Stockholder's Equity. For these last two I will enter not just the most recent numbers, but I will need to enter the prior year numbers as well."

"Did you say this is how rating agencies do it?" Hannah asked.

"This is only a very rough approximation. They use much more sophisticated models in addition to a lot of non-quantitative or qualitative information. This model is one that only uses available financial data and is not all that accurate, but it is the best I've got."

Nobel busied himself entering the data as Hannah turned to Cy. "What do you think you are going to do?"

"I really don't know. I suppose I will just have to wait and if the company were to go under perhaps I could go in and purchase it through bankruptcy reorganization. Perhaps I could restore it to its former self."

Figure 6-1
(Left side of spreadsheet)

Rate-Determining a

Copyright © 2007, 2011, 2013 AC

www.BusinessAllst

	Name		Garbenzoa-Tech
	Account	End Yr	Beg Yr
1	Sales	250,524	
2	EBIT (Net Operating Income)	16,055	
3	Interest Expense	9,860	
4	Net Income (cont oper) [NI]	708	
5	Depreciation Expense [DE]	16,638	
6	Cashflow from Operations (CF)	19,042	
7	Capital Expenditures (CE)	19,759	
8	Long-Term Debt [LTD]	144,465	
9	Total Debt [TD]	231,734	229,306
10	Stockholder's Equity [SE]	198,586	199,607

"Aren't you a little suspicious of the finance types that you suspect have been offering up numbers and information to the public that is self-serving? Besides, where would you get the financing?"

"I made enough when I was removed from the company to be in a position to take advantage of a super low stock price. I also know of quite a few employees that would step up with resources."

"There," Nobel said.

"How accurate do you think this thing is?" Cy asked.

"I've been using this model for several years and found that it is pretty good.

"Out to the far right and at the bottom it indicates that the approximate bond rating would be a 'B'." Is that right?" Hannah pointed out.

Bond Rating

BA - All Rights Reserved

tars.com

Date

Calculations	Ratios	Rating	#
EBIT / Int Exp	1.63	B	
EBITDA / Int Exp	3.32	BB	
(NI + DE) / TD	7.5%	CCC	
(CF - CE) / TD	-0.3%	CCC	
EBIT / avg (TD + SE)	3.7%	CCC	
EBITDA / Sales	13.1%	CCC	
LTD / (LTD + SE)	42.1%	BB	
TD / (TD + SE)	53.9%	BB	
Approximate Bond Rating		B	

"That's right, it calculates several ratios from the data that was entered and compares the results to a predetermined profile. Then, from that profile it assigns a rating to each ratio. As you can see, the various resulting ratings range from BB to CCC. The result is the average of all the ratings."

"That is pretty interesting," Hannah noted.

"Just as I suspected," Said Cy.

The Reality

"How would you use this information?" Hannah asked.

"Bond ratings are divided into two classes. Those that are AAA, AA, A, and BBB are called investment grade bonds. Those that are BB, B, CCC and so on are called non-investment, high-yield or junk bonds. If this analysis is correct then the company is in the non-investment category and should command a high interest rate. It also means they are highly risky and more susceptible to failure," Nobel pointed out.

"What interest rate should they pay?" Hannah wanted to know.

"That all depends on the current economic climate and what the markets are demanding. It changes all the time. If the company were rated as AA when they first issued the bonds and had a rate of say 4% the current market rate could change even though the company might not. It all has to do with money supply, economic growth expectations and things like that. The rate could go up to 5% for new bonds issued by the company at a AA rating. It could even go down to 3%."

"Of course if the financial conditions within the company change that could also change the market expectation. My calculation suggests the financial condition of the company is now B and so would definitely require a higher interest rate."

"Is there any way of knowing what that current market rate would be?" Hannah continued.

"I have another model."

"I should have expected such."

Nobel opened another model on his computer. "I will do a quick survey of what existing bonds that are rated B are paying. I select about fifteen B-rated

178

companies and enter their current market rates. Then from another source I enter what AAA bonds are paying. I use a 10-20 year time frame to look at longer term bonds.

Figure 6-2
(Complete spreadsheet)

Bond-Determining Corporate Bond Rates
Copyright © 2007, 2011 ACBA - All Rights Reserved
www.BusinessAllstars.com

Name				YTM %	Bond Rating	Spread
Corporate Bonds			Date			
B	AAA					
7.677		1		3.06	AAA	0.00
7.813		2		3.70	AA	0.64
10.714		3		4.48	A	1.42
7.738		4		5.46	BBB	2.40
7.727		5		6.77	BB	3.71
7.738		6		8.65	B	5.59
7.854		7		11.69	CCC	8.63
10.689		8		18.23	CC	15.17
7.692						
8.989						
8.713						
8.238						
9.705						
8.600						
9.852						
Y-axis 8.649	3.060					
X-axis 3	8					

"There is a predetermined relationship between bonds in the various classes from AAA to CC. From my calculations it shows B bonds current market rate at 8.65% and AAA bonds at 3.06%."

"Boy that is quite a difference," Cy noted.

"It really is," Nobel added.

"Is there any way to check the current status of the market to see how close these numbers are to reality?" Hannah asked.

179

"There are various services that show what the last trade of these bonds was sold at and with what expectations." Nobel went to a web page and a service that provided the data. "It looks like they are still rated AA with an interest rate of 3.5%."

"How is it possible the market could miss this discrepancy? I was always under the assumption the market is pretty efficient and factors in all the relevant information," Cy wondered.

"It is pretty good about large companies, but sometimes the very small companies don't have people watching them very close. For whatever reason they seem to have missed this one," Nobel pointed out.

"What is our next move?" Cy wanted to know.

"I think we just wait. Unfortunately, if we advise anyone to sell the stock and it depresses the price, we could be complicit in trading on insider information. We know what is going on, but will just have to bide our time."

"What about all those employees who have their retirement tied up a plan that has purchased company stock and can't get out of it?" Cy complained.

"I don't know what to tell you. Maybe we are wrong. We will just have to keep an eye on it and see what happens."

"It is interesting to know that we have this information, but can't do anything about it," Hannah felt frustrated.

Nobel looked at Cy and just shrugged.

Sometime later that week, Cy left the following message for Nobel: "Company just announced that it is going into chapter 7 bankruptcy."

When Hannah saw the message she asked Nobel, "What does chapter 7 mean?"

"Chapter 7 bankruptcy is where a company stops all operations and goes out of business. A trustee is appointed by the court to liquidate the company's assets and the money used to pay off any debts."

"That seems pretty radical."

"It is a death nail. It differs from a chapter 11 that allows the business to reorganize their business affairs and assets in such a way so they can meet their debt obligations. In a chapter 13 the debtor must reorganize the company finances under the supervision of the courts and submit a plan to repay all debts using most of the income from the company for repayment. I think you could safely say the company was murdered."

"Who did it? Was it the venture capitalists that changed the operations to maximize the bottom line? Was it the rating agencies that did not pay close enough attention and gave the company a good report card when it didn't deserve it? Was it the new management of the company who just couldn't make everything work?"

"It is a complex problem. It might have been the market itself that moved away from the products the company was providing and the company did not adjust. There could even have been new competition that compromised the company's ability to succeed."

"One thing we know: there were definitely problems in how the bonds were rated," concluded Hannah.

Nobel turned to Hannah. "You are amazing. You have a real talent for this stuff."

Hannah just smiled.

Summary of Concepts

Bonds

"A debt investment in which an investor loans money to an entity (corporate or governmental) that borrows the funds for a defined period of time at a fixed interest rate. Bonds are used by companies, municipalities, states, and U.S. and foreign governments to finance a variety of projects and activities. Bonds are commonly referred to as fined-income securities. The indebted entity (issuer) issues a bond that will be paid and when the loaned funds (bond principal) are to be returned (maturity date). Interest on bonds is usually paid every six months (semi-annually).[12]"

Rating of debt

"A bond rating is a grade given to bonds that indicates their credit quality. Private independent rating services such as Standard & Poor's, Moody's and Fitch provide these evaluations of a bond issuer's financial strength, or its the ability to pay a bond's principal and interest in a timely fashion. Bond ratings are expressed as letters ranging from 'AAA', which is the highest grade, to 'C' ('junk'), which is the lowest grade. Different rating services use the same letter grades, but use various combinations of upper- and lower-case letters to differentiate themselves.[13]"

---

[12] http://www.investopedia.com/terms/b/bond.asp
[13] http://www.investopedia.com/terms/b/bondrating.asp

CBUD

Learning Objectives

An understanding of:
New Project Questions
Cash Budget 12-Month Model
Capital Budgeting Model
Benefit to Cost Ratio (BCR)
Internal Rate of Return (IRR)
Net Present Value (NPV)
Discounted Payback (DPB)
Real Options

Spreadsheet Tools found at
www.businessallstars.com/calculator

Assessment found at
www.businessallstars.com/assessment

The Last Resort

Nobel sat in the large open foyer of the resort hotel on a rustic sofa that was intended for lounging guests. He looked out through the massive windows that displayed the beautiful scenery the resort was known for. It was so good to get away from all the work. He had grown accustomed to Hannah being at his side and sharing in their various adventures. He felt relaxed, but he did miss her.

It was brunch time and a few guests were mingling about near the front desk and the concierges counter. Other than that it was surprisingly quiet except for three young women who sat at a table some distance to his left.

They seemed oblivious to the wonderful view and the other guests as they chatted, laughed and enjoyed each other. He wondered what conversation was so interesting that they were not relaxing as he was and just soaking up the atmosphere.

Suddenly, he heard a bell ring and looked over to a place near the front door to see a woman in a resort uniform holding a clip board. She announced that the morning hike and tour were about to leave and anyone who had signed up should assemble just outside the front doors.

He stood and walked past the woman, through the doors and found four people sitting on the edge of the rock planter box beside the doors. Two more people were standing on the opposite side of the entryway. A woman came walking up the front steps. She was obviously the guide wearing hiking boots, oatmeal socks, brown shorts, tan shirt and floppy nature hat. He wondered if this was the total group for the hike when the doors opened behind him and the three women appeared.

The guide counted the people in attendance and announced: "Ten, it looks like we are all here."

"Is it going to be very strenuous?" asked one of the seated hikers.

"It's close to a two mile hike and will take us about an hour. I don't think it is anything you can't handle," she said as she surveyed what everyone was wearing. "It looks like everyone has good shoes and I hope you've brought sun screen and bug spray."

One of the seated women raised her arms to show a plastic container in each hand. "Ready," she announced. "I've got enough for everyone."

"Good, then let's go," announced the guide as she turned and headed across the concrete porch toward the trail head.

Nobel was concentrating on following the person in front of him when all at once he was aware that one of the young women from the joyful trio was walking beside him.

"Excuse me, but we were in the session you taught titled 'Show Me Your CBUD,' and were very impressed," she said.

"Oh, thank you," he responded, moving his focus from the women to the trail and back again.

"As a matter of fact we have a few follow-up questions. Do you think you might have some time we could bend your ear?"

He looked forward to see the guild leading the group up the trail. "Give me one of your questions."

"We are the ABCs, I'm Abby, this is Brea and that's Cat," she said motioning to the two women who followed.

He turned to acknowledge them.

"We work for Unihyben, Inc. a major corporation in the hybrid energy field that is always looking for new ideas and opportunities to diversify. We are a team that has taken a week to get away, do some brainstorming and take in your seminar. We think we have discovered a brilliant idea and need to know how to present it to management." "Unfortunately, we are all science-slash-engineering types and are not sure how to communicate our concept most effectively. We were interested in the steps you mentioned in your seminar and how they might apply to our project."

Nobel became aware the hikers had come to a halt and glanced toward the guide. She was looking back to see that all the hikers were together then turned and was off again. "Well, the first step is to answer the twelve questions."

Twelve Questions

"Every company has a non-quantitative component of a request for funding. They are intended to answer Who, What, When, Where, How, and Why. I have compiled a set of twelve questions that summarize many of the most common points investors will ask. The first step in any request is to address these issues," he offered.

"What are the questions?" Brea interjected.

"Well, let me roll through them quickly:"

The Twelve Questions:

1. What business are you in?
2. What is your strategy?
3. What market needs will you serve?
4. How is the product pricing set?
5. Where is the product in its life cycle?
6. Identify skills, processes, and branding?
7. How big is the market and will it grow?
8. Who is the competition?
9. What generates competitive advantage?
10. How will the market be reached?
11. What skills do key individuals bring?
12. What is the potential risk of failure?

As he completed the list the group came to a clearing and overlook where the guide stopped. Identifying various points of interest and natural phenomena, the group was very attentive. As they resumed hiking Abby once again saddled up beside her mentor. "Can you tell me more about the questions?"

"Let's take these one at a time and you give me your best response," he instructed as they hiked along. *"What business are you in?"*

"We are in the energy business, but more specifically we are focusing on electricity generation," she responded. Her two companions listened carefully close behind.

"Okay, *what is your strategy?"* he continued.

"We want to find a cost effective hybrid solution to electrical generation using natural elements," she declared.

"That sound like a worthy goal. *What market needs will you serve?"*

"The demand for electricity in the Orlando, Florida area," she added.

"Why Orlando, if I can ask?"

"That is the highest concentration of lightning in the United States."

"Lightning," he mused.

"That's right."

"Okay, *how is the product pricing set?"*

"That is a difficult one. We anticipate it will be competitive with existing rates. It will be slightly more expensive in the initial years, but as the result of government subsidies it will be fairly transparent to the end user."

"Where is the product in its life cycle?" he asked.

"We observed a situation where lighting propelled a weight some distance. As a result of that, we developed a system that will draw lightning to a central area and through the use of gravity, store the power generated for distribution on a demand basis. In the Orlando area there are as many a fifty strikes per square mile per year."

"Identify skills, processes, and branding. What I mean by this is, will you have any proprietary positions?"

188

"Absolutely, our patent is in the final stages of approval and once we gain exclusive rights to the geographic areas selected, we will have a powerful position from which to operate."

"How big is the market and will it grow?"

"Our first...." she began before being interrupted by the guide.

"We will stop here and observe a unique feature of natural terrain in this area," the guide observed while she gathered the group around her. She continued her instruction as Abby, Brea, and Cat surrounded their mentor. Nobel could sense their energy, enthusiasm and excitement and drew strength from them. The guide continued her dialogue, but his mind began to wonder about this new venture the women were proposing.

When the group moved forward Abby was once again at his side. "As I was saying, our first site will be in Orlando, Florida because of the potential there, but if our technology proves successful and economically feasible for other locations we will be able to expand at an exponential rate. We believe it is and will be." she pressed.

"Who is the competition?" he asked.

"I think that goes without saying, it is all the utility and energy companies in the area."

"What generates competitive advantage?" he continued.

"We will be so far out in front of other potential replicators, with state of the art systems that it will be hard to catch us," she noted.

"How will the market be reached?" he continued.

"This is an interesting one. We would go out on our own, except the corporation we work for and who would be funding us, has an extensive network in place.

We would leverage their connections and marketing strength."

"What skills do key individuals bring?"

"I am an electrical engineer, Brea is a mechanical engineer and Cat is a meteorologist. We all have bachelor's degrees and two of us have master's degrees. We each average about eight years of professional experience and have worked together as a team on several projects before. We are very compatible," she said with pride.

"What is the potential risk of failure?" he queried.

"That is a hard one. We are all very optimistic, but realize that natural elements are not very dependable. We have factored in a normal distribution of potential outcomes and feel that under typical conditions all signs are very positive. In addition to that, we have run extensive tests on our models and prototypes. The technology works extremely well. There are risks, but we feel the potential for failure is remote," she said confidently.

The guide stopped the group and said: "This next section is going to be very interesting; I will be stopping you quite often so pay close attention to the fascinating features of this amazing habitat."

The group completed the hike with little more interaction regarding the project the women were proposing. As they concluded the hike the three women approached their mentor as they entered through the resort front doors. Abby asked him, "So where do we go from here?"

"Well, I have a luncheon meeting with the seminar directors and meetings this afternoon."

"Will you be at the social this evening?" Brea asked.

"I think so."

"Good," the three women said in unison.

He felt flattered by the attention they offered.

The Two-Step

He walked into the large convention room that had been converted into a dinner dance hall with orchestra and bar. It was crowded and dark, but he was greeted by several of the organizers who gave him directions. He decided to work his way toward the bar for a drink and moved stealthily through the people. When almost to his destination he felt a tug on his arm.

He turned around and there were three extremely attractive women in stunning evening dresses. It was Abby, Brea, and Cat. "We have a table if you'd like to join us," Cat offered.

"Sure," he replied and followed them to a table in the corner.

As they sat down he spoke up so they could hear him above the music, "Why would three attractive women want to spend the evening with me?"

"We have ulterior motives," said Brea.

"You don't think you're worthy of our attention?" questioned Abby.

"Listen, I'm happy to help you, but why don't we just enjoy the evening. I have some free time tomorrow if you would like."

"That would be great," intoned Abby.

They ate, laughed and genuinely had a good time. At one point Abby wanted to dance and so she pulled him to the dance floor. Before they could get started all three women were dancing with him.

The next day the four met at a small table on the resort veranda. As they were settling in he said, "Yesterday on the hike we discussed the Twelve Questions. I'd like to follow up with those for a moment. In the first place you only answered with brief off-the-cuff explanations. Your formal report will need to go into much more depth and justification. So don't think a quick answer will suffice."

"How much depth are you talking?" Cat asked.

"You need to really sell this proposal, but also be prepared to offer solid and defendable answers to very penetrating questions about every aspect of your write-up," he replied."

Cash Budget 12-Month Model

"Now the second step is to prepare a 'Cash Budget 12-Month Model' for the first year. This will require you to think through all the possible revenues and expenses associated with the project. I force my clients to do this to make them think through the detail. There are a lot of versions of these forms that could accomplish this task, but I use a form that is simple and quick. You must enter information into assumption boxes and the rest of the form flows from there," he clarified as he opened his laptop and turned it on.

"I don't know if we have all the answers right now," Brea offered with concern.

"That's okay. We will go through the process and you can massage the data later when you get better information. We will use a preformatted spreadsheet."

"The top third of the sheet (Figure 7-1) is where you will enter the assumptions," he said as he clicked the mouse several times and a form appeared on the screen.

"There are four rows of data that are required.

"The first is where you will enter the total initial investment dollars requested and the life of the project. What will be the upfront dollars needed?"

"We will need about five million dollars for all the equipment. What do you mean by the life of the project?" Cat added as she examined the form.

Figure 7-1
(Left side of spreadsheet)

CASH Budget 12-Month

Copyright © 2009, 2011, 2013 ACI

Investmnt: [ ] Life: [ ] Depr:

	Rev	COS	Sal/Wages	Benefits	Prof Fees	Travel
$/unit						
$/mon						

Months	1	2	3	4	5	6
Units sold						

"How long will the equipment last before it is worn out and needing major updating? The IRS has guidelines for assets and how long they will last. These are general depreciation parameters. They are grouped into classes from 3, 5, 7, 10, 15 or 20 years. Which life would you think most applicable to your equipment?"

"I would hope it lasts forever, but I know that is unrealistic. I would guess that a five year life is the most appropriate," Brea responded.

"Whatever life we enter will generate a percent for depreciation the first year. The next item to enter is the percent of the total initial investment that will be required each year for renewals and replacements. This is an estimate for ongoing additions to fixed assets. It is followed by the cash conversion days and finally the applicable income tax rate," he said as he pointed to the format.

The women all huddled close to see the screen and follow the pointer as he moved it around. "What do you mean by cash conversion days?" Cat asked.

Figure 7-1 (continued)
(Right side of spreadsheet)

ı Model - Year #1
3A - All Rights Reserved

R/Repl %:	Days:	Tax %:

Rent	Utilities	Supplies	R&D	Marketing	Other

7	8	9	10	11	12

"I need to get a fix on how much working capital you will need to support the project. To do this we need to estimate your policy for holding inventory, collecting from customers and paying bills. Let's assume you hold inventory for 30 days before it is sold and then it takes you another 20 days to collect from the customer. That is 50 days of credit you will have to finance. If you pay for that inventory by delaying payment for 40 days, that shows up on the books as accounts payable, then you only need a net 10 days of credit."

"I don't think there will be any inventory that we purchase from anyone and so there won't be inventory days or payables days. I assume we would be very similar to our parent corporation where the average customer pays in 20 days."

"Excellent, we are off and running. The next row is where we enter the variable amounts. Do you see the shaded box with the heading Rev?" he pointed to the screen.

"The two boxes under that heading relate to your Revenue assumptions. All the rest of the boxes in those

195

two rows under the various headings are for expense assumptions. The first row captioned '$/unit' is for entering variable dollars per unit and the second row captioned '$/Mon.' is for entering the fixed dollars per month."

Units Per Month

"The last row in this assumptions section is where we enter the units for each month. Why don't we start with that row and work back to the variable and fixed," he offered.

"Sure," Abby conceded.

"Tell me how many units you anticipate selling each month during the first year of operations," he instructed.

"We anticipate the charge will be about six dollars per kilowatt hour and we will sell about 80,000 kilowatt hours the first month of operation," Cat estimated.

"You see our project is not just a lightning harvester. It is a hybrid system that will gather energy from solar and wind as well," Brea added.

"We don't need to be exact for this first round, just give me some rough estimates," he said.

"Well, if I talk in terms of thousands, let's go with 80, 160, 250, 250, 400, 500, 500, 500, 400, 200, 200 and 160 for the first year," Abby offered.

"Great," he said and as she said each number he entered it into the row for "Units."

"You didn't enter the whole number. You dropped the thousands," Cat interjected.

"That's right we don't need to go crazy with detail at this point. Numbers without the trailing "000" will be fine."

Revenue Assumptions

He continued: "Now let's go back and look at the rows just above units. You said you would charge $6.00 per kilowatt hour. We will enter the 6 in the first column after $/unit. Do you think there will be any revenue earned that will not come from a direct charge for hours?"

"What do you mean?"

"Will you generate any revenue that is unrelated to kilowatt sales?"

"We don't anticipate any," Brea said.

"Because Revenue is all variable and not fixed I will put the 6 in the first row and a zero in the second or $/mon. row. Now for the expenses," he continued.

	Rev	COS	S/W	E/B
$/unit	6			
$/mon	0			

"So the $6 is not in thousands," Cat queried.

"That is right. We will enter the $/unit at full value but the $/mon. in thousands," he pointed out.

"That seems a little confusing," the women seemed to say in unison.

"The $/unit end up in thousands when multiplied against the units, but the $/mon need to be in thousands because they will be added to the result."

"I think I get it," expressed Cat.

Expenses Assumptions

"We need to go through each expense column now and determine the variable and fixed portion of each. Let's start with COS or the Cost of Sales. Will you be purchasing anything that will be resold?"

"If I understand what you are saying, I will offer my opinion. We will need to purchase some electricity to supplement that which we generate as our final product. So there will be some Cost of Sales," Abby explained.

"Can you put a dollar value on it?"

"I think $1 per kilowatt hour will be purchased," Abby added.

"So it will be all variable and you won't routinely purchase anything on a monthly basis, irrespective of unit sales," he declared.

"That's right," Brea confirmed.

	Rev	COS	S/W	E/B
$/unit	6	1		
$/mon	0	0		

"We will put $1 in the first row for $/unit and a zero in the second row for $/mon. under the heading for COS. The next two columns are S/W for Salaries and Wages and E/B for Employee Benefits. Can you tell me how many people will be involved?"

As the women began to discuss amongst themselves their mentor interjected, "Now we are talking about incremental people."

"What do you mean, incremental?" Cat asked.

"We want to include only those costs that change as a result of this project. If there are people in the corporation that were there before and will be there whether we do this project or not, then their cost is not incremental. We only want to look at what changes because of the decision to go forward with this project."

"We will be hiring quite a few new positions for the project at a combined cost of around $960,000 per year."

"Are they salaried or hourly?" he inquired.

"They will be on salary, but we will need additional support on an hourly basis."

"What do you estimate that cost to be?"

"I would think about $2 per kilowatt hour," Abby added.

"We will enter $2 under S/W across from $/unit and then $80 across from $/mon. I think that will cover it," he said.

The women studied the form closely. "$80 for the fixed per month plus $2 times 80 units will equal the first months salaries and wages of $240,000. I think I'm beginning to get it," Cat noted.

$$\textit{Fixed plus variable = first month S/W}$$
$$\$80 + (\ \$2 \times 80 \text{ units }) = \$240$$

"Closely related to the Salaries and Wages is Employee Benefits. A lot of people think that if they offer no benefits to employees they should enter a zero. This is wrong because every employee must pay FICA and Medicare tax which the employer matches, unless they are independent contractors. So as a minimum the E/B will be around seven and one half percent of S/W. Workmen's Compensation would be added to that and then anything the company offers would be an addition. For Salaried Employees this could be as much as forty percent of Wages," he pointed out.

"I guess I never realized that," Brea chimed in.

"Let's put $.30 into the variable and $24 into the fixed," stated Abby.

"Sounds good," added Cat.

	Rev	COS	S/W	E/B
$/unit	6	1	2	.3
$/mon	0	0	80	24

"Now I want you to think about each of the other expense categories such as Fees which are Professional Fees to accountants and lawyers, Trav. for required travel costs, Rent and Util. for Utilities. Make the same analysis of Sup for Supplies, R/D for Research and Development expense, Mkt. for Marketing and Othr for any other costs and expenses we haven't included."

"You must try and determine any and all incremental costs the company will have to add because of this project."

"This is getting pretty detailed," Cat noted.

"That's right we want to make sure we cover all the bases," he encouraged as he stood up. "I need to make a call and then I'll be right back.

The women huddled around the computer and made their best estimates in each box of the expense categories for the two rows.

When he returned the women were sitting back in their chairs and discussing the various assumptions they had made. He looked at the computer and saw that they had filled out the boxes that needed input. "It looks like you have made your estimates."

"We gave it our best shot," Abby responded.

"You will need to really nail down all the assumptions before your final formal presentation," he instructed. "Now, the middle section of the form (Figure 7-2) is where the assumptions generate that detail by combining all the fixed and variable for each revenue and expense."

"For example, Salary and Wages for the first month ended up as 240 or two hundred and forty thousand dollars."

That is the result of 80 kilowatt hours of energy sold times a variable salary rate of $2 per hour or $160,000. To clarify once again, we add that to the $80,000 of fixed salaries and get the combined $240,000.

Variable rate times units
$2 x 80 = $160,000

Variable plus fixed equals total
$160,000 + $80,000 = $240,000

"Each column and row in this section is the result of both a variable and fixed amount being added together. If there was no variable then it is only the fixed and vice versa."

"There are two rows that are subtotals. One is the Gross Profit where Cost of Sales is subtracted from Revenue. The other is EBITDA where all the expenses are subtracted from the Gross Profit. It is called EBITDA because it is the Earnings Before Interest, Taxes, Depreciation and Amortization."

"If you looked at some row and felt the calculation did not accurately reflect what was going to happen you could override it with a direct input, but I hope you would highlight that so someone reviewing the document would be aware of that change."

The women examined the middle section. "The EBITDA really jumps around doesn't it?" Cat offered.

"Well, that is directly related to the seasonality of your units and how the calculations flow."

Figure 7-2
(Left side of spreadsheet)

CASH Budget 12-Month
Copyright © 2009, 2011, 2013 ACE

Investmnt: $ 5,000.00   Life: 5   Depr: 20.0%

	Rev	COS	Sal/Wages	Benefits	Prof Fees	Travel
$/unit	6.00	1.00	2.00	0.30	0.00	0.00
$/mon	0	0	80	24	20	20

Months	1	2	3	4	5	6
Units	80	160	250	250	400	500
Revenue	480	960	1,500	1,500	2,400	3,000
Cost of Sa	80	160	250	250	400	500
Gross Pr	400	800	1,250	1,250	2,000	2,500
Sal/Wages	240	400	580	580	880	1,080
Benefits	48	72	99	99	144	174
Fees	20	20	20	20	20	20
Travel	20	20	20	20	20	20
Rent	40	40	40	40	40	40
Utilities	8	8	8	8	8	8
Supplies	20	36	54	54	84	104
Res/Dev.	26	42	60	60	90	110
Marketing	56	104	158	158	248	308
Other Exp	68	116	170	170	260	320
EBITDA	(146)	(58)	41	41	206	316

"Why did you say we need this form?" Brea asked.

"Someone investing funds in this project will want to know how the cash will flow."

"They will want to be able to anticipate in which months there will be a cash drain or a cash surplus."

All major corporations are very aggressive when it comes to cash management and this will help in that effort."

Figure 7-2 (continued)
(Right side of spreadsheet)

Model - Year #1
3A - **All Rights Reserved**

R/Repl %:	5.0%		Days:	20	Tax %:	25.0%

Rent	Utilities	Supplies	R&D	Marketing	Other
0.00	0.00	0.20	0.20	0.60	0.60
40	8	4	10	8	20

7	8	9	10	11	12
500	500	400	200	200	160
3,000	3,000	2,400	1,200	1,200	960
500	500	400	200	200	160
2,500	2,500	2,000	1,000	1,000	800
1,080	1,080	880	480	480	400
174	174	144	84	84	72
20	20	20	20	20	20
20	20	20	20	20	20
40	40	40	40	40	40
8	8	8	8	8	8
104	104	84	44	44	36
110	110	90	50	50	42
308	308	248	128	128	104
320	320	260	140	140	116
316	316	206	(14)	(14)	(58)

"If this was a standalone project and you were going to a bank, they would expect a form like this and not only that, they would expect the first three years to be charted so they could know when you would be short of funds and may need a line of credit and in which months that might be repaid."

Figure 7-3
(Left side of spreadsheet)

EBITDA	(146)	(58)	41	41	206	316
Work Cap	316	316	355	-	592	395
Renew/Repl adj:			63			63
Depr Tax Shield:			(63)			(63)
Taxes:			41			(141)
Net Cash	(462)	(374)	(292)	41	(386)	125
Cum Cash	(462)	(835)	(1,128)	(1,087)	(1,472)	(1,348)

Total Units:	3,600	**Var Cost per Unit:**	
Revenue per Unit:	6.00	**Fixed Cost:**	

"Look at the third section of the form (Figure 7-3) at the bottom. We've taken the EBITDA and subtracted addition non-operating cash needs such as W/C+ for Working Capital Increases and R/R+ for additional Renewals and Replacements of Fixed Assets."

"The Working Capital increase each period is the result of how many 'Days' of credit we entered at the top. When we entered 20 days of credit we said that inventory days plus accounts receivable days less accounts payable days were a net 20 days. We will have to extend net credit for that many days of revenue. So we take the monthly revenue and divide that number by 30.41667 or the average number of days in a month to find the revenue per day and then multiply that times the 20 days."

Revenue per day
$480,000 / 30.41667 = $15,781

Daily revenue times credit days
$15,781 x 20 = $316,616

204

Figure 7-3 (continued)
(Right side of spreadsheet)

316	316	206	(14)	(14)	(58)
-	-	(395)	(789)	-	(158)
		63			63
		(63)			(63)
		(210)			22
316	316	873	775	(14)	141
(1,032)	(716)	157	932	918	1,059

4.90	IC changes:		881.23
2,808	IC % of Rev:		4.1%

"The resulting $316,616 is the net working capital we will have on our books for the first month. Each month after that, we add or subtract the incremental change."

"The renewals and replacements number is the result of multiplying the total investment times the percent we entered at the top, which is an estimate of how much additional we need to invest in fixed assets each year."

Additional investment each year
$5,000,000 x 5% = $250,000

Quarterly purchases
$250,000 / 4 = $62,500

"The Tax/S stands for the tax shelter that depreciation expense provides. Depreciation is a non-cash expense and so it is not included in our form, but it does reduce how much taxes we will pay in a period. When we entered the $5,000,000 total investment at the top and the related 5 year life it generated the 20% that was to be depreciated in the first year.

First year's depreciation expense
$5,000,000 x 20% = $1,000,000

Taxes shelter from depreciation
$1,000,000 x 25% = $250,000

Quarterly tax savings
$250,000 / 4 = $ 62,500

Lastly, there is Taxes for payments to the government."

"The last two lines are for C/F (the net Cash Flow) and CUM stands for the cumulative cash flow. The first is for a one month number and the second is to show the result of adding the current and all previous months together," he said.

"I see that in the fifth month we are down almost one million five hundred thousand in negative cumulative cash flows, but by year end we are up over a million," Abby noticed.

"The summary data at the bottom will help us as we move forward to step three. It shows the total units for the year, the revenue per unit, variable cost per unit, and the total fixed cost for the year. In addition, it shows the total added to IC (Invested Capital). It is a summary of the incremental change shown in W/C+ and R/R+ rows for the year. It also shows the IC change as a percent of the total year's revenue." he summarized.

206

A Little Diversion

Just as he was clicking on the screen to bring up the next spreadsheet Cat motioned toward a far balcony of the resort. It was higher than the veranda they were sitting on and some distance away in a remote location. "Do you see that," she pointed out.

The rest of the group turned and focused on the distant extension from the building. A man in his mid-fifties was looking off into the distance had both arms extended with hands grasping the railing. "That looks like our CEO Mr. Howard," Abby noted.

"I think it is Mr. Howard," Brea added as she leaned a bit to the right. "I think the only thing he has on is little speedo."

The group all looks a little closer. "Not terribly attractive," said Cat. "You know, last night at the dance I thought I saw him at a table with a young woman, but I convinced myself it couldn't be."

"What was she like?" asked Abby.

"Like that," Cat nodded toward the balcony. An attractive brunette in her mid-twenties walked out of the suite and joined Mr. Howard.

"Did I miss the sign somewhere that said this was a topless resort?" asked Brea.

"I hope she has sunblock on because that would be the only thing covering her," the mentor said. "It kind of makes it hard to continue with the CBUD analysis."

"So the guy wants to get away with his wife for a little R and R. Isn't that okay?" interjected Brea.

"I've seen his wife and that's not her. As a matter of fact I think that's Ms. Havital from budgeting," Cat clarified.

"Is she the CPA that we have to submit our proposal to for a first run through, review and prioritization?" Abby asked.

"I'm afraid so," Cat admitted.

Suddenly, the three women all jumped up from their chairs and scrambled to the seclusion behind an overhang as the couple on the balcony looked in the direction of the veranda. Their mentor remained seated returning his attention to the computer as he clicked several times and then closed up his device. He slowly got up and without paying any attention to the distant couple, picked up his things and made his way toward where the women were standing. "I don't think we are going to get anything more done right now. I've got a meeting in a few minutes anyway."

"Can we continue later?" Abby pleaded.

"Sure, what works for you?" he scanned the trio.

"What are you doing for dinner?" Cat asked.

"I guess I'm going over CBUD with you."

Getting Down to Business

He walked into the resort restaurant and wondered if he had the time and place wrong. He walked around and then spotted the three women huddled at a table behind a large planter. Abby motioned for him to join them and as he approached he realized the little alcove where they were seated was quite secluded.

"We didn't want to be noticeable in case Mr. Howard and Ms. Havital happened to come in," Brea explained.

"Boy have we got things to tell you," Cat said excitedly.

"I hope it is about the inputs to our next schedule," he responded.

"Well, It's concerning what we found out this afternoon about our great CEO," Abby reconciled.

"I don't want to be too distracted, can we hold any discussion about your CEO until after we do a little work here," he resolved.

"Oh, sure enough," Brea jumped in.

He opened up his laptop and busied himself getting everything ready. The women sat patiently until he finally announced, "I have opened up another predesigned spreadsheet that is the heart of the capital budgeting proposal."

The women leaned in close to see the screen.

"This model has three parts. The first is at the top and where we will enter all of our assumptions. The middle will automatically calculate the operating cash flows, once all the assumptions are filled in. The bottom generates information about incremental net operating and invested capital needs, the net salvage value, and finally the free cash flow for each year."

Figure 7-4
(Left side of spreadsheet)

	CBUD - Capi
	Copyright © 201

	A
Initial depreciable investment:	
1st year units:	
Sales price per unit:	
Variable cost per unit;	
Deprec (3,5,7,10,15 or 20):	
Tax Rate:	
NOIC chng. % of Revenue:	
BCR	**IRR**

"We need to begin by focusing on all the assumptions that are required. The worksheet is designed with the assumptions separated out in this way so that if we were to do any what-if analysis it would be easy to change a few things and see the total impact."

"What is the purpose of this form," Abby asked.

"This form will generate a five year free cash flow projection so that we can do a benefit to cost analysis."

"It will force us to estimate what our initial cost will be and then forecast what future benefits will follow. Every request for funding and resources has to offer the company a promise of a return. It is easy to ask for dollars today, but it is more difficult to project what the benefits will be," he noted.

Figure 7-4 (continued)
(Right side of spreadsheet)

tal Budgeting Model
1 ACBA - All Rights Reserved

ssumptions

		Initial Non-Depr. Investment:		
Growth:				
		Inflation Assumption:		
		First Year Fixed Cost:		
0.0%	0.0%	0.0%	0.0%	0.0%
		Salvage Value:		
		Weighted Avg Cost of Capital:		

NPV	DPB

"That gets really difficult. It was hard enough projecting the first year units on a month by month basis. Looking out five years seems almost impossible to me." Cat admitted.

"How else is management going to know if they should spend the money? We need to enter seven inputs in the first column and six in the very far right column (Figure 4-5). On the second row we will enter growth as a series of percentages for each of the years."

"Several of the inputs will come from the Cash Budget – Twelve Month Model that we just prepared. For example we know the initial investment of $5,000,000 and 5 year life of the project. We know the first year units as 3,600, the sales price per unit of $6.00 and the variable cost per unit of $4.90."

Figure 7-5
(Left side of spreadsheet)

CBUD - Capital Budgeting Model	
Copyright © 201:	
	A:
Initial depreciable investment:	5,000.00
1st year units:	3600
Sales price per unit:	6.00
Variable cost per unit;	4.90
Deprec (3,5,7,10,15 or 20):	5
Tax Rate:	25.0%
NOIC chng. % of Revenue:	4.1%
BCR 1.11	**IRR** 13.6%

"We also know the tax rate of 25% and the Net Operating and Invested Capital percent of revenue at 4.1%."

"The first year fixed cost of $2,808 that is entered in the far right column also came from the Cash Budget. We also need to enter an assumption in the first box of that column for our initial depreciable investment. How much money will you need to purchase fixed assets before the operations actually begin? In other words how much money do you want management to give you to get this thing going?"

"We need about five-million dollars to acquire our site and all the equipment we will need," Brea stated.

Figure 7-5 (continued)
(Right side of spreadsheet)

Name:	Unihyben		

1 ACBA - All Rights Reserved

ssumptions

	Initial Non-Depr. Investment:			0
Growth:	5.0%	5.0%	5.0%	5.0%
	Inflation Assumption:			3.0%
	First Year Fixed Cost:			2808
20.0%	32.0%	19.2%	11.5%	11.5%
	Salvage Value:			1000
	Weighted Avg Cost of Capital:			10.0%

NPV	671	**DPB**	4.72

"Going back to the years of depreciation: everything we are doing here is on a cash basis and so rather than use the depreciation methods that generally accepted accounting principles offer, we will use what the IRS allows. What we actually pay the IRS in taxes is the real cash impact. They use a system called the Modified Accelerated Cost Recovery System or MACRS. We can select from 3,5,7,10,15 or 20 years. Which one of those most closely represents the life of your most expensive equipment?"

"I would think about 5 years," offered Cat.

"Great, as we enter that into the sheet we will see that depreciation percentages will automatically appear to the right for each of the five years."

Figure 7-6
(Left side of spreadsheet)

BCR	1.11	**IRR**	13.6%
			0
Initial Investment			-5000
Units Sold			
Revenue			
Variable Costs			
Fixed Costs			
Depreciation			
EBIT			
Taxes			
NOPAT			
Depreciation Add Back			
Operating Cash Flow			
Net Operating Working Capital			
Working Capital based on Rev			
Cash flow due to NOWC			-885.6
Salvage Value			
Salvage Cashflow			
Book value of asset			
gain or loss on sale			
taxes on gain or loss on sale			
Net cashflow on salvage			
Net Cashflow			-5885.6
			-5885.6

Figure 7-6 (continued)
(Right side of spreadsheet)

NPV	671	DPB	4.72	
1	2	3	4	5
3600	3780	3969	4167	4376
21600	23360	25264	27323	29550
-17640	-19078	-20632	-22314	-24133
-2808	-2892	-2979	-3068	-3160
-1000	-1600	-960	-576	-576
152	-210	693	1365	1681
-38	52	-173	-341	-420
114	-157	520	1024	1261
1000	1600	960	576	576
1114	1443	1480	1600	1837
958	1036	1120	1212	0
-72	-78	-84	-91	1212
				1000
				288
				712
				-178
				822
1042	1365	1395	1508	3870
-4938	-3811	-2762	-1732	671

"In the last column the first input is for initial non-depreciable investment. Will there be any upfront

215

purchase for equipment, land or other items that will not depreciate?"

"I don't think so," stated Brea.

"Now for the growth rates, how much will the units grow from year to year over the course of five years?" he asked.

"We are trying to be conservative here. I think if you enter 5% for each year that would be extremely reasonable," offered Brea.

"Five percent it is then. I would think a 3% inflation assumption should go into the third box in the far right column. Is that okay?" he said.

"Sure, who knows what inflation will be," Abby responded.

"The two last items are for the Salvage Value and the Weighted Average Cost of Capital. These get a little more interesting."

"What do you mean by Salvage Value?" Cat asked.

"This is the dollar amount the whole project could generate if sold after five years," he explained.

"Sold?" Brea was confused.

"If you were to close down the project and sell the equipment after five years, how much could you get for everything?"

"I don't know maybe a million, but why would we do that?" Abby questioned.

"The other option is to enter a horizon or terminal value representing all future cash flows."

"This would also basically be what the project was worth at that point and if you sold the business, what someone would pay for it at fair market value."

"If we are successful, that could be a lot of money," Abby stated.

"That is true, it could be millions. Let's be conservative and just enter the million for now. The last item is the cost of capital."

"What is that?" Cat asked.

"That is the financing cost for the corporation to generate dollars to invest in projects in their company. It represents a combination of borrowed money and new equity. Whatever percent we enter will be the discount rate we apply to the project to bring the future cash flows back to present value. "It is a hurdle rate or the required rate the company must generate to cover the cost of those financing dollars."

"Oh the hurdle rate, when I was talking to George he said the corporation uses a 10% hurdle rate. Do you mean that is the rate we must clear to make this a go?" Cat inquired.

"That's right."

"Why don't you look over the assumptions and see if I've entered everything in such a way that you understand it," he instructed.

The women examined the sheet, carefully comparing numbers to the Cash Budget sheet and to the notes they had been taking. "It looks just like we discussed except for the last row at the bottom. What are all those numbers?" questioned Brea.

"Those are the metrics that have been calculated as a result of the assumptions and the worksheet they generated. I would like to hold the discussion of those for a few minutes, if that is okay?"

"Okay," Cat acquiesced.

"Now the next thing we are going to do is examine the second portion of the worksheet. Here (Figure 7-7) is where the operating cash flows are calculated. Each year the units time the revenue rate gives us the total revenues. Inflation will increase the rate from year to year and the units will increase as a result of the growth rate."

"Variable cost will also increase as the rate is adjusted for inflation and the units grow. The Fixed Costs will change from year to year only because of inflation. Depreciation for each year is the result of multiplying the initial depreciable investment times the depreciation percent for that year."

"When we subtract all the costs from the revenue we get the EBIT or Earnings Before Interest and Taxes for each year. We then multiply EBIT times our tax rate to generate the tax amount that is subtracted from EBIT leaving us with the NOPAT or Net Operating profit After Taxes. Then we add depreciation back to get the Operating Cash Flow."

"Why do we add depreciation back? We just subtracted it," Brea asked.

"We treated it as a cost because it will reduce our taxes. Once the tax is calculated, we add it back because it is not a cash expense."

"That's a little confusing," Cat offered.

"If we didn't include depreciation then our taxes would be higher and our operating cash lower. So we have to factor in the impact of depreciation somehow and this is how I've elected to do it. Let's move on to the third part of the form or the bottom piece. Here (Figure 7-8) is where we will bring it all together. Two things happen that many people find confusing."

"We need to adjust our cash flows for net operating and invested capital. Two of them are the adjustment to assets for working capital and incidental fixed asset changes and the other is for the salvage value or horizon value."

"The Salvage value is money that comes in at the end of the project, but if it is greater than the book value of the assets we have to pay taxes on any gain."

"Remember for NOIC we only adjust for the change and for Salvage Value we get the money less any taxes on the gain. We build up Net Operating and Invested Capital over the life of the project, but in the last year we get it all back." he emphasized.

"Are we going to have to calculate this?" Cat asked.

"Not really. The worksheet does it all for you, once the assumptions have been entered. I just wanted to give you a little explanation of what was happening. The result is that we get a bottom line which is the Net Cash flow for each year."

"These are critical numbers that will be used in our evaluation of the project."

Just then Abby nudged Brea and nodded toward the main area of the restaurant. They all looked up to see Mr. Howard and Ms. Havital enter the eating area and be seated. "It sure is strange to see them with clothes on once you've seen them the other way. I don't know if I'll be able to get that picture out of my mind once we get back to the corporation," Cat said.

"We have a lot to tell you about what we found out," Brea seemed to burst forth.

"About what?" he finally surrendered.

"Well, we have been doing a little snooping and found out that Mr. Howard comes here once every quarter. The last few times it has been with Ms. Havital," Cat offered.

"He comes and has meetings with three guys in very exclusive closed door sessions," Abby continued.

"How do you know all this?" the mentor asked.

"We have been talking to a couple of the staff that we have become close to. They love to talk because even though Howard throws money around like its water, he is very cheap when it comes to tips and the staff. As a matter of fact he is a real jerk, to quote one guy." Cat said.

"I know this is all very intriguing and I can see you all are fascinated, but it really has nothing to do with your project and its potential for success," he responded.

"We are not so sure," Abby replied.

"I've only got a little more time before my afternoon meetings and I did want to go over the next step with you.

When You're in a BIND

"The next step is to calculate the decision metrics that appear at the bottom of the assumptions section (Figure 7-6). I like to calculate four that are pretty universally used. They are the Benefit to Cost Ratio that many academics and text books call the PI or Profitability Index. The next is the IRR or the Internal Rate of Return that shows what discount rate would make the project breakeven. This is followed by the NPV or the Net Present Value which shows all of the future cash flows discounted back to the present and subtracted from the initial investment. The last is the DPB or the Discounted Payback. This last metric shows how long it will take to recover the initial investment using discounted future cash flows."

Not all companies use all of these and some companies may use a few others, but the four that are calculated are pretty standard. There is some debate regarding the validity of the various measurers but, that aside, we will calculate them and show how to use them. We will start by listing the free cash flows from the bottom of the last section (Figure 7-5) that we just reviewed. Out to the left (Figure 7-6), we will indicate in which year the cash flow occurred."

"In the second column we will enter the present value of each of the amounts from the first column. To do this we will apply the discount rate and the time frame over which it is to be discounted. We will use the formula:

$$PV = FV / (1 + WACC)^{Year}$$

Figure 7-6

Cumulative Discounted Cash Flows
WACC
10.00%

	Cash Flows	Disc. Cash Flows	Cum. Cash Flows
0	-5886	-5886	-5886
1	1042	948	-4938
2	1365	1127	-3811
3	1395	1049	-2762
4	1508	1030	-1732
5	3870	2403	671

"PV stands for the present value to be calculated, FV stands for the future value from column one, and the WACC is the discount rate, the Year is an exponent for how many times the preceding number in parenthesis is used. For example the third number would be:

$$\$1,127 = \$1,365 / (1.10)^{2}\text{"}$$

"The last column is the cumulative discounted cash flows and is the result of adding the current year number to the prior accumulation. So in year two the sum of all prior years would be a negative $4,938. If we add $1,127 to that we will find that after two years the project is only down a negative $3,811. The last number in that column is the sum of all the discounted cash flows and is the Net Present Value of $671. You can see it in the last row of the assumptions section (Figure 7-6)."

"This means that the discounted benefits exceeded the initial investment by 671 thousand dollars. To find the benefits we add the NPV to the initial investment and divided the benefits by the initial investment. So the Benefit to Cost Ratio would be:

Cost plus NPV over Cost
$$1.11 = (\$5,886 + \$671) / \$5,886"$$

"The Internal Rate of Return is a little more difficult to find. It is the rate that will make the present value of the benefits exactly equal the initial investment or where the NPV is zero. To find this we can either us a special function in the spreadsheet or just keep adjusting the discount rate in the form we are currently using until the NPV becomes zero. If we do this we will find (Figure 7-7) the IRR to be 13.6%."

"Through this process we have found the first of the three metrics. The last one is the Discounted Payback Period or DPB. We find this by referring back to the original 10% WACC form (Figure 7-6) and scanning down the far right hand column. We see that the cumulative discounted cash flow turns positive sometime in the fifth year. So the DPB is four year plus some portion of the fifth year. To find that fraction we divided the absolute value of the last negative cumulative discounted cash flow by the next years discounted cash flow. We do this as in the following:

Portion of the year calculation
$$.72 = 1,732 / 2,403"$$

Figure 7-7

Cumulative Discounted Cash Flows
WACC

		13.6%	
	Cash Flows	**Disc. Cash Flows**	**Cum. Cash Flows**
0	-5886	-5886	-5886
1	1042	918	-4968
2	1365	1059	-3910
3	1395	953	-2957
4	1508	907	-2050
5	3870	2050	0

"We add the .72 to the four we just identified and get 4.72 years until the project pays back its initial investment. If the final cumulative discounted cash flow is negative, the project never pays off the initial investment and the discounted payback can't be determined."

"Comparing each of the numbers with some standard (Figure 7-8), for example:

Figure 7-8

Metric	Decision Rule
BCR	Greater than one
IRR	Greater than WACC
NPV	Greater than zero
DPB	Less than the Life

224

Figure 7-9

	Cash Flows	Disc. Cash Flows	Cum. Cash Flows
Cumulative Discounted Cash Flows			
WACC			
10.00%			
0	-5886	-5886	-5886
1	1042	948	-4938
2	1365	1127	-3811
3	1395	1049	-2762
4	1508	1030	-1732
5	3870	2403	671

"As you can see this project is favorable for each of the measurements when compared with their respective decision rule. If the assumptions are correct, then we would recommend the project be approved. The only problem is that it may have to compete with other projects the company is considering that also have positive results. In that case a ranking will occur based on one or more of the metrics. With limited funding the company may only commit to a few projects and those with the highest BCR, IRR, or NPV would be selected. Sometimes projects with lower ranking metrics will be funded for reasons that are not altogether financial. They may have a strategic advantage or be required to keep existing facilities operational, such as a new furnace."

"I think our numbers are pretty good and they certainly fall within upper managements thrust for dramatic new growth opportunities," noted Brea.

Their mentor checked his watch. "I've got to leave for now and have one last step to discuss with you. What do you think?"

"When will you be out of your meetings?" Cat asked.

"I'm afraid not until four o'clock," he responded.

"We have a few things to follow up on, could we meet at five?" Abby put forth as she looked for confirmation from the other women.

"Five would be fine," he responded.

"There is a deck by the pool on the south side. Would that be okay?" Cat added.

"Sure, by the way, how long are you staying?"

"We are leaving tomorrow morning, just before noon, how about you?" Abby asked.

"I'm leaving first think in the morning, so this may be our last chance to wrap things up."

What Options Do We Have?

He heard their laughter before he ever saw them. As he turned the corner he spotted the three sitting in their swim suits around a deck table under a large umbrella. "I think you are enjoying yourselves why too much," he noted.

"You won't believe what we have uncovered," Cat offered.

"Our Mr. Howard is quite the suspicious character," Brea added.

"Don't tell me you've been doing more snooping?" he queried.

"We have so much to tell. He meets every quarter with three guys, one an attorney, Mr. Wendell and the other two, Mr. Waring and Mr. Wyatt are heads of companies we do major business with," Abby informed.

She continued. "Not just two other companies, but we did a search on the internet and found they are principles in at least a dozen companies that have some financial connection with the corporation we work for."

"Did you ever hear of Enron?" asked Cat.

"You're not telling me this is connected to Enron?" He asked with surprise.

"No, but it looks like the same kind of set up. The guy at the top of Enron was taking profits from ownership positions in companies that were doing business with Enron," chipped in Abby.

"We suspect the same thing is happening here," Brea followed-up.

"Do you have any evidence?"

"Not yet, but it certainly smells like a rat," Cat added.

"You know what happened to Enron. When the fraud was detected management sold their stock before it plummeted. The employees were legally locked out of selling until the price was at rock bottom. Do you want to start a scandal like that?" he asked.

"Not really," Brea concluded.

"If all of this is speculation and you have no proof, you could even be hurting your own careers."

There was a long pause and then the mentor offered, "Speaking of options, that is the last step. Have any of you ever purchased an option?"

All three of the women shook their heads to acknowledge they had not. "I have to disagree with you. Each of you buys an option every month. If you purchase insurance on your home, car or health you are buying an option. If you don't have a claim the option expires unexercised and you are out the premium cost of the option. But if you have a claim, you exercise your option and the insurance pays up. Options are a critical part of how business works."

"I never thought of it that way before," Cat admitted.

"I'm going to ask you a few questions and see if your proposal is subject to real options analysis. Is that okay?"

They all agreed.

"How critical is it that your project be done this year and can it be delayed a year?" he asked.

"Not without affecting some of our costs," responded Cat.

"It would benefit us in one way, we would have better information about a bill before the state legislature," added Brea.

"What bill is that?"

"There is a proposed bill that will come up next year in the state senate that could hurt us if it passes," Brea offered.

"That leads to the second question: Is there some external event over which you have no control that could materially affect your proposal?"

"I would say the bill is the big thing, not counting the possible exposure of Mr. Howard," Abby clarified.

"Without the bill our volumes would most likely be five percent higher or 3,800 units in the first year. If the bill passes the volumes would drop to around 3,400. What we did was to average the two for our proposal and got 3,600," Cat noted.

"It looks like you have treated it as a fifty-fifty proposition that the bill will pass. That was the third question: what are the chances the external event will happen? So the downside from waiting is that the cost of your initial investment could go up, but by waiting you would have better information about the possibility of success?"

"That about sums it up," Said Abby.

"What if you were to buy an option that would allow you to lock in today's prices with the sellers of your equipment for a year and then just wait? How much would you be willing to pay?"

"We have no idea," Brea spoke for the group.

"Let's try something I'm going to bring up the format for the CBUD or the Capital Budgeting Model and enter all the original assumptions except for the units. Then I will enter the upside units. What did you say they were?" he asked.

"Enter those units in the form (Figure 7-10), while leaving everything else the same and see what the metrics show." He entered the data. "It looks like all of the metrics are greatly improved. Now I'm going to change the units to 3,400 in the form (Figure 7-11) and see what the results are. Not only are the metrics much worse, they all appear to be below each of their decision rules."

229

Figure 7-10
(Left side of spreadsheet)

CBUD - Capital Budgeting Model
Copyright © 2011

	A:
Initial depreciable investment:	5,000.00
1st year units:	3800
Sales price per unit:	6.00
Variable cost per unit;	4.90
Deprec (3,5,7,10,15 or 20):	5
Tax Rate:	25.0%
NOIC chng. % of Revenue:	4.1%
BCR 1.23	**IRR** 17.1%

"We figure 3,800 units," Brea responded.

"That is amazing," Cat noted.

"What a power tool for changing one input while holding everything else constant," said Abby.

"If we wait one year for perfect information we see that we could either elect to go ahead and generate an NPV of $1,375 or if it's negative then do nothing."

"Do nothing?" Brea questioned.

"That's right, if the units are going to be down, then the NPV will be negative $32 and rather than go ahead we would elect not to proceed with the project."

Figure 7-10 (continued)
(Right side of spreadsheet)

Name:	Unihyben			
ᴵ ACBA - All Rights Reserved				
ssumptions				
	Initial Non-Depr. Investment:			0
Growth:	5.0%	5.0%	5.0%	5.0%
	Inflation Assumption:			3.0%
	First Year Fixed Cost:			2808
20.0%	32.0%	19.2%	11.5%	11.5%
	Salvage Value:			1000
	Weighted Avg Cost of Capital:			10.0%
NPV	1375	**DPB**	4.47	

"Interesting," said Cat.

"If we multiply $1,375 by 50% and zero by 50% and add the results we will have an expected NPV of $687.5.

Upside select and downside don't
($1,375 x .50) + (0 x .50) = $687.5

"That is an improvement over the $671 from our original proposal."

Present value of NPV
$687.5 / 1.10 = $625

231

Figure 7-11
(Left side of spreadsheet)

CBUD - Capital Budgeting Model	
Copyright © 201:	
	A:
Initial depreciable investment:	5,000.00
1st year units:	3400
Sales price per unit:	6.00
Variable cost per unit;	4.90
Deprec (3,5,7,10,15 or 20):	5
Tax Rate:	25.0%
NOIC chng. % of Revenue:	4.1%
BCR 0.99	**IRR** 9.8%

"The only problem is the $687.5 is one year out and so to make them consistent in today's dollars we discount the $687.5 by our discount rate of ten percent and get $625."

Improved NPV by waiting
$671 - $625 = $25

Subtracting $625 from the $671 we see that we can improve our position by $46,000 if we wait for perfect information. That is the value of waiting and that is the maximum you would be willing to pay the sellers of the equipment for an option to freeze the prices for one year."

Figure 7-11 (continued)
(Right side of spreadsheet)

Name:	Unihyben			

L ACBA - All Rights Reserved

ssumptions

	Initial Non-Depr. Investment:			0
Growth:	5.0%	5.0%	5.0%	5.0%
	Inflation Assumption:			3.0%
	First Year Fixed Cost:			2808
20.0%	32.0%	19.2%	11.5%	11.5%
	Salvage Value:			1000
	Weighted Avg Cost of Capital:			10.0%

NPV	(32)	DPB		

"That's really interesting," Abby said. "Is there more?"

"There is a lot more, but that gives you the basics."

"Why don't you go and get your swim suit on and we will all get in the hot tub and then eat out here?" Cat instructed.

"Sounds like a plan. I'll leave my laptop here for you to play with and be right back," he said.

The Big Question

He sat at his desk reviewing the days email when the phone rang. On the other end was a woman's voice, "This is Abby. Can you meet with us, we have something extremely important to discuss with you?"

"I'd like to but you are only 700 miles away," he responded.

"No, we are here in town. We flew in just to meet with you."

"Well, in that case, I'd better make time, when and where?"

"Can we come to your office in about an hour?"

He checked his schedule, "I have a couple of things, but I will clear the schedule. That is the least I can do."

The three women came into his office and found seats around a small conference table in one corner. They were smartly dressed, but their usual joy seemed to have vanished. "This must be quite serious," he stated.

"It is," Cat said. "We can absolutely prove that Mr. Howard is up to his ears in fraudulent behavior and when it is reported the company is going to go down."

"That could be the death nail for our project, unless we go out on our own," added Brea.

"But more important than that are the employees and their retirement accounts that are heavily invested in company stock. When we expose the double dealing all of our friends and associates will lose everything," Abby offered with concern.

"Is there any way they can get out of company stock before this comes to light?" he asked.

"Is that ethical?" Cat wondered.

"Is it legal?" Brea enjoined.

"If they all start dumping the stock, won't the price fall anyway?" Abby added.

"I think you have a tiger by the tail," their mentor exclaimed. "Does it need to be all or nothing?"

"What do you mean?" asked Cat.

"What do you know about the chairman of the board?"

"His name is Hoolahan and as far as we can find determine he is also involved," Abby added.

"Let's take another approach. Who are the major stockholders?"

"The employees own about 30% of the stock in an Employee Stock Ownership Plan. The next largest stockholder is the State retirement system with about 15% of the stock," explained Brea. "Then there is some guy by the name of Watanabe who owns about 10%."

"We will start with Watanabe. I will approach him and then contact the head of the state retirement system. I will keep your identity confidential. If we can get a few powerful players on our side we may be able to transition this thing and keep it from collapse. You know I think this project of yours and a few others like it just might be the salvation of the company."

Over the course of the next several months the following headlines appeared in the financial news:

Unihyben, Inc. stock tops $54

Howard resigns as Unihyben CEO
Unihyben, Inc. stock drops to $30

Hoolahan out, Watanabe in as Unihyben. board chairman

Unihyben, Inc. stock @ $38

Unihyben, Inc. sees growth in new lightning project
Unihyben, Inc. stock reaches $49

Three women are new VPs at Unihyben

Summary of Concepts

The Twelve Questions:
1. What business are you in?
2. What is your strategy?
3. What market needs will you serve?
4. How is the product pricing set?
5. Where is the product in its life cycle?
6. Identify skills, processes, and branding?
7. How big is the market and will it grow?
8. Who is the competition?
9. What generates competitive advantage?
10. How will the market be reached?
11. What skills do key individuals bring?
12. What is the potential risk of failure?

Working Capital Needs: Estimate your policy for holding inventory, collecting from customers and paying bills. Let's assume you hold inventory for 30 days before it is sold and then it takes you another 20 days to collect from the customer. That is 50 days of credit you will have to finance. If you pay for that inventory by delaying payment for 40 days, these show up on the books as accounts payable, then you only need a net 10 days of credit.

Fixed and Variable: The first row captioned '$/unit' is for entering variable dollars per unit and the second row captioned '$/Mon.' is for entering the fixed dollars per month."

Units per Month: How many units do you anticipate selling each month during the first year of operations?

Incremental: We want to include only those things that change as a result of this project.

Cash Budget 12-Month Model: Prepare a Cash Budget 12-Month Model for the first year. This will require you to think through all the possible revenues and expenses associated with the project. I force my clients to do this to make them think through the detail.

Employee Benefits: Closely related to the Salaries and Wages is Employee Benefits. A lot of people think that if they offer no benefits to employees they should enter a zero. This is wrong because every employee must pay FICA and Medicare tax and the employer must match that. So as a minimum the E/B will be around seven and one half percent of S/W. Workmen's Compensation would be added to that and then anything the company offers would be an addition. For Salaried Employees this could be as much as forty percent of Wages.

OPTIONS

Learning Objectives

An understanding of:
Real Options
Expected NPV
Maximized NPV

Spreadsheet Tools found at
www.businessallstars.com/calculator

Assessment found at
www.businessallstars.com/assessment

On Her Own

Hannah and Mario were relaxing on the rear deck to her home when detective Hammersmith and Sergeant Rice appeared at the back gate that came from Nobel's home.

As Hammersmith came through the gate he called out to Hannah. "Do you know where Merchant is?"

"He is away on vacation. I think he went to some mountain resort. He was very secret about the whole thing. I don't think he wanted anyone to bother him."

Approaching the deck the detective continued, "Do you know when he'll be back?"

"I suspect by the end of the week. What seems to be the problem?"

"I've got a case that may need his expertise."

"Can I be of any assistance?"

"I don't know."

"Why don't you tell me the particulars and just as soon as he arrives, I'll fill him in," Hannah instructed as she gestured for the detective and sergeant to sit in the two empty chairs that completed the grouping around a low table.

"Have you heard of the case of Ophelia de la Fontaine?

"No, was it in the news?"

"It has been about six weeks ago. She was murdered in her apartment by strangulation. We don't think it was sexual assault or robbery and are running out of leads."

"Who was she?"

"She had been very involved in modern dance theater in her younger days, but for the last ten years she owned Ophelia's costume shop just on the fringe of the downtown area," Sergeant Rice offered.

"She had been married four times, but was divorced from her last husband and was living alone. Her business which primarily focused on ballet and modern dance costumes seemed to be floundering some in the last year," Hammersmith added.

"Do you have any suspects?"

"No, we have exhausted all possibilities. Each of her previous husbands are all living out-of-state and have been accounted for. Her business associates and personal contacts have all been removed from suspicion. We've been through her customer lists and can't find any reasonable leads. The crime scene is completely clean and there are no witnesses in her apartment building that can identify anyone coming or going at the time of the murder. We are at a dead-end."

"Wow, why do you think Nobel could help?"

"I don't know. He has been very unique in his approach to a few cases we have had a hard time with and I'm just trying anything I can think of."

The conversation continued with a few social graces and then the detective and sergeant excused themselves.

"What do you think?" Mario asked.

"I don't know," Hannah paused. "I have a few friends in the modern dance field. I think I'll do some noodling around before Nobel gets home."

"Do you need any help?"

"I think I'll be okay."

The next day, Hannah found herself at the modern dance building at the University. She went to the office of Professor Grandeur and knocked. No one answered and then a student came walking by and said the professor was probably in class. Hannah checked her watch and as she turned the professor was coming down the hall. "Gwen," Hannah said.

"Hannah, how good to see you. It's been too long since I've seen you. What are you up to," the professor said as she approached her door with key in hand.

They went into Gwen's office and sat down. "A lot has happened, but most recently I've been working with a fellow who has been consulting with the police on various criminal cases."

"Oh really," Gwen seemed taken aback. "What about the modeling?"

"I think I've moved on from that and found a new love in my life. I'm not referring to a person, but an interest in finance."

"You've got to be kidding."

"No, it is really strange. The way my neighbor, Nobel Merchant has been mentoring me has really peeked my curiosity. I think I've always had some capability in math, but this had become very exciting for me."

"I'm amazed."

"Well, the reason I'm her is a person by the name of Ophelia de la Fontaine."

"Oh yes, Ophelia…what a tragic thing."

"Did you know her?"

"Oh yes. She was very involved in the dance department for years. Most recently she has provided some of the costumes we have used in various productions."

Just then a woman appeared at the door and interrupting the two interjected, "Have you been over to the Stepson building yet?"

"No I am going in just a few minutes," Gwen replied.

"Let me know what you think," the woman said and was gone.

"I'm sorry for the interruption, but that was our department chair and she gets a little hyper sometimes. We are looking at a temporary space in a suburban building for a satellite training facility."

"Oh really," Hannah was curious. "When will all this happen?"

"It is still on the drawing board. We are only exploring our options. It is an old building and we can only get a five year lease, but it is perfectly located in an area where there are a lot of residential students living. It would also serve our extension program for high school students."

"I'm fascinated. You say you're going out there now?"

"Yes, I have an appointment with the building manager in about half-an-hour. I'm afraid I need to be going."

"Would you mind if I tagged along?"

"Not at all, we can catch up on old times on the way."

As they drove Hannah brought the conversation back to the murder. "It is just tragic about what happened to Ophelia."

"I agree, she was always such a pleasant person."

"I often wonder why anyone would want to do such things to another person."

"You know the police have interviewed almost everyone within the department. I spent almost an hour with them."

With this last comment, Hannah realized that she might be retracing old ground. Finally, they arrived at a large suburban parking lot. The building had once been a local supermarket built more than fifty-years ago. Most recently, the large cavernous space had been used for various purposes. They met Stan Speckelford, the building manager and who was waiting at the door fronat.

"Now you realize we can only go with a five years lease. The owners are planning on a complete redevelopment of this area and don't want to commit to anything longer than that." Speckelford insisted.

"We are a very bureaucratic group and this decision might not happen for another year," Gwen acknowledged as she wandered around the large open space. "We would want a five year lease from the time we actually sign, which could be a year from now. On the other hand we would be an excellent tenant."

"I'm going to have to talk with the owner's."

Hannah stayed by the building manager as Gwen explored the area. "What was in here before?" Hannah asked.

"Most recently it was a fabric store," the man said very curtly.

Gwen returned from her examination. "I think I've seen everything in here. We would cover the cost of all the improvements to convert this space for our purposes."

"Sure," Stan acknowledged.

After the inspection the Gwen thanked Stan for his attention. As the two women were driving out of the parking lot Hannah noticed Alice's, a women's and children's apparel shop in the strip mall next to the building. For some reason it peeked her curiosity.

After leaving the university, Hannah drove back out to the apparel shop. As she pulled in she looked at the façade, the signage, and the appearance more critically. The shop seemed to be making its best effort to survive, but was not wildly prosperous.

244

She went in and noticed there was no one in the shop except for a middle aged woman that was sitting behind a counter. The woman stood up and addressed Hannah. "Can I help you?"

"I'm interested in your shop."

"What do you mean?"

"I should say, I'd like to visit with the owner of the shop. Is Alice around?"

"That's me."

"My name is Hannah Watson and I wonder if you've ever thought about selling the shop." She didn't know why she said that, but it just seemed to come out.

"I've considered it from time to time...why?"

"Let me ask you a different question. Have you ever met a person by the name of Ophelia de la Fontaine?"

The woman became immediately more cautious. "What is all this about?"

"I don't know. I just had this feeling that you might have met her."

"I might have. How are you connected with her?"

"I'm just someone who is interested in her and concerned about her untimely death. You did now that she has passed away."

"I read about it in the newspaper."

Hannah was totally on a fishing expedition. Based on a wild guess that Ophelia, not doing well at her current location and aware of the university's interest in the old building was interested in relocating. Could she have seen the shop and made an offer to purchase the operation? She now realized she probably should have been more devious in her approach, but the cat was out of the bag.

"I think she might have approached you with an offer to buy you out."

"That is a pretty bold assumption."

"Just tell me yes or no."

"What if she did," the woman responded.

Bingo, Hannah had taken a wild leap and it paid off. "Let me ask you a different question. Are you aware that owners of this site are thinking about a total redevelopment in the next five to six year?"

"They have conveyed that to me."

"Was Ophelia aware of that?"

"I don't think we need to pursue this conversation any further. If you want to purchase a dress, we can talk about that, but that is all," the woman said with firmness.

"I apologize if I've been a little abrupt and nosey. I really don't mean to offend you. It's just that a crime has been committed and someone is getting away with murder. Anything you could do to help solve this terrible misdeed would really be appreciated. I'm going to leave my telephone number and if you want to talk any further, please call me." Hannah took out a piece of paper and jotted down her name and phone number. "Thank you for your time," she said as she handed the paper the Alice.

As Hannah drove home from the dress shop she began to wonder how serious Ophelia had been about moving to the new location. She decided to make a detour and go downtown to where Ophelia's costume shop was located. Her GPS directed her to a side street several blocks from the high-rise buildings of the main business district.

She found a place to park and walked to the shop. There was a large sign in the window that read: "Going out of business sale." Another sign in smaller letters indicated: "Everything 30% to 70% off." As she entered the front door, Hannah saw a young woman inside serving a customer. She busied herself until the customer left and the clerk was alone.

"May I help you?" the clerk asked.

"My name is Hannah Watson and I'm interested in the circumstances surrounding the tragic death of Ophelia."

"Are you with the police?"

"No," Hannah offered.

"Are you from the news media?"

"No, I'm just a friend."

"Oh, well how can I help you?"

"I'm not too familiar with the business that she ran her. Can you tell me anything about it?"

"As you can see we are going out of business. I almost wonder if Hannah anticipated this. You see, several months ago she didn't renew her lease."

"Did the shop do pretty well?"

"Not really. I've been here for about a year and in that time we've struggled. I don't know if it's our location and we are too far from the performing arts theaters and the university. Ophelia tried to continue to be very active in that realm, but things seemed to be moving away from her."

"Did she ever mention moving the shop to a different location?"

"I think she was trying to do that, but I don't know where."

When the conversation was finally ended Hannah returned to her car and drove home.

Nobel Returns

It was late Friday night when Nobel returned from the mountains. The next morning he was late getting up and wandered into the kitchen. At the sink he looked out the window and saw Hannah reading on her back deck. He was excited to tell her about his adventure with the three women and so he wandered out the back door and over to her house.

"Your back," Hannah acknowledged as Nobel came through the gate. "How was everything?"

"I thought it was going to be more relaxing that it ended up being."

"Why, what happened?"

Nobel spent the next hour rehearsing all the events of the past week. He explained the CBUD capital budgeting approach that he uses and how the three women had used it. Hannah was a very attentive audience. He showed her the spreadsheet models and how they worked and what the implications were for their use.

When Nobel was finally concluding his demonstration, he asked, "Has anything happened around here?"

"Not much, just another murder detective Hammersmith wants you to look into."

"What!" Nobel burst forth.

Hannah then proceeded to disclose the details the detective had left and continued on with her own investigations. "I don't think the police even know about the building the modern dance department at the university is thinking about leasing. Nor do they know that Ophelia was seriously looking to move her shop to be adjacent to the proposed site."

"You are amazing," Nobel admitted.

Just then the phone rang and Hannah answered it. She continued a conversation for a few moments and when she hung up, turned to Nobel. "You're not going to believe this, but that was Alice from the shop Ophelia was thinking about buying."

"I thought you said she was rather cool toward you."

"She was, but suddenly she wanted to talk and asked if I'd come back and talk with her."

"Any idea what it is about?"

"A guy came to her shop and wants to buy it, but rather than an outright purchase, he wants to secure an option to purchase it in the future."

"Really, that sounds very interesting."

"I told her we would come out later today. What do you think?"

"I guess we're going to see her."

Later that day Hannah introduced Nobel to Alice at her shop. It was right at closing time for a Saturday, which was 5 pm. Alice locked the front door and then the three sat around a small table in the back of the shop.

"I've never seen this guy before and suddenly he comes into my shop, knows all about my operation and proposes to buy an option on the shop."

"What did he say?" Hannah asked.

"He said he would pay me $5,000 right now for the right to purchase the shop anytime in the next twelve months for $100,000. The $100 thousand would be a firm price and not subject to change and I could keep the five thousand no matter what happened."

"I would propose we calculate what the value of that option is really worth," Nobel interjected.

"I don't understand."

"The reason he wants to delay his decision to purchase your shop is to see what happens with the university and their decision to occupy the building next door. He wants to lock down the price now and then wait until he has better information before moving ahead."

"Can he do that?"

"Sure, if you agree to his terms."

"I'm not sure what to say."

"You say you have never seen this guy before."

"That's right. He said his name is Gus Kunz and he is looking to get into this market for dance apparel. The strange thing is the price he offered is exactly the same price the Ophelia had proposed. She wanted to move forward right away, but this guy wants this fancy option."

"How very interesting," Hannah pondered.

"If you can give me some numbers, we can determine how good his offer is."

"You mean the $5,000 could be low?"

"That's right. It is always good to know what we are dealing with. I'm going to pull up a little spreadsheet to work from. It allows us to enter some assumptions and determine if his price is good."

"That would be wonderful."

"Can you tell me what how much cash you generated this past year from operating the business?"

"After subtracting all my expenses, a salary for myself and some assistants and income taxes, and subtracting what I had to pay for a new computer, I generated about $10 thousand in cash."

"Did you include any depreciation as an expense?"

"Yes, my accountant said I need to recognize about $10 thousand in depreciation on store fixtures and leasehold improvements."

"If I add that depreciation back because it is not a cash expense, then you actually generated a positive $20 thousand in cash flow."

"Well, that is probably right."

"If the university doesn't add a dance facility next door, what would you project your cash to be each year for the next five years."

"We don't grow very much, but I would say you could increase that by about $2 thousand each year."

"I'm going to enter negative $100 thousand in period 0 for the downside cash-flow, $20 thousand for period 1 and $22, $24, $26, and $28 thousand for each of the next four years. What do you think would happen if the university moved forward with their plans and did the dance extension?"

"To be wildly optimistic, I would estimate we could grow by almost $20 thousand each year."

"Really," Hannah wondered.

"Yes, a facility like that would bring in a steady stream of traffic and if we stocked the right kind of products, we could do quite well."

"I'm going to enter the same negative $100 thousand in time period zero and then $20, $40, $60, $80 and finally $100 thousand for five years." Nobel turned to Hannah and asked, "Did your contact at the university say what the odds were they will move forward with the extension?"

"She said it would be about fifty-fifty."

"I'll enter that as the upside probability. The spreadsheet will automatically take the difference between that and 100% for the downside. I'm going to assume your cost of financing is about 20%. That is a combination of interest costs and the return you expect on your ownership. I'll enter the 20% in the cell that is labeled WACC, the 50% in the upside probability, and 12 months in the 'Months to decision'."

Figure 8-1

REAL OPTIONS ANALYSIS
Copyright © 20013 ACBA - All Rights Reserved
BusinessAllstars.com

Name	Alices Shop		Date	

Time Period	Cashflow Upside	Cashflow Downside		
Period 0	-$100.00	-$100.00	(Period 0 cashflow must be negativ	
Period 1	$20.00	$20.00		
Period 2	$40.00	$22.00	WACC	20.00%
Period 3	$60.00	$24.00	Upside Probability	50.00%
Period 4	$80.00	$26.00	Months to decision	12
Period 5	$100.00	$28.00		Best NPV
Period 6				times Prob.
Period 7				Discounted
Period 8			Upside NPV	$23.76
Period 9			Downside NPV	$0.00
Period 10			-----	
-----			Maximized NPV	$23.76
NPV	$57.93	($30.38)	Expected NPV	$13.78

			Real Option Value	$9.98

"This program calculates a normal net present value for both the upside and the downside projections. Just as in the time value of money it discounts all cash flows at the WACC or the weighted average cost of capital of 10%. The result is that in today's dollars the upside generates a positive $57.93 thousand above the cost of $100 thousand. The downside ends up with a loss of $30.38 thousand. So the future cash benefits are less than the original $100 by that amount."

"Clearly the upside is a better course," Hannah noted.

"That is right, but we are dealing with an option to defer actually doing either of these for one year until we have perfect knowledge of some external event. That event is the dance extension. If it comes in we will go ahead and spend the $100 to buy the shop and reap the positive NPV. If the extension doesn't come in, we would forego purchasing the shop and not end up with the negative $30.38 thousand."

"So by paying for the option now someone could lock in the purchase price and either move forward or walk away one year from now," Hannah observed.

"That's Mr. Gus Kunz' intent," Nobel said.

"What are all these other calculations?" Alice pointed to the spreadsheet.

"There is a line called the 'Expected NPV' which is the weighted average of the two normal NPV's we just calculated. Fifty percent of the upside NPV plus fifty percent of the downside NPV equals the weighted average or the expected NPV:

$57.93 x .50 =	$28.97
($30.38) x .50 =	($15.19)
Expected NPV	$13.78

"If Ophelia were to go ahead and purchase the shop today for $100 thousand she would expect on average to generate $13.78 above her cost. That is in today's dollars. But if someone, like Gus could pay a small fee and wait until he had perfect information he might be able to improve his position."

"Do you see the figure of $23.76 that is labeled 'Upside NPV'? Let me tell you how that is calculated. At the end of twelve months, knowing what direction the university will go, Gus could either go ahead with the purchase or walk away. He has two options. If the university opens the extension then Gus would buy the shop and end up with the $57.93 NPV. If the university decided not to open the shop Gus would walk away and not suffer the negative $30.38. He has just improved his position by waiting. By waiting he has pushed his NPVs out twelve months and so he has to bring them back that same period. We divide the WACC by twelve to get a monthly rate and then take one plus the monthly rate for the designated number of months. The monthly rate would be 20 divided by 12 or 1.6667."

$57.93 / (1.01667)^{12} =$	$23.76
$0 / (1.01667)^{12} =$	$0
Maximized NPV	$23.76

"The result is a weighted average of what we would do under either situation is a maximized NPV. The result if $23.76. We have improved our position by $9.98 or almost $10 thousand by waiting to make the decision until better information is known."

"From this analysis and the assumptions you have given me, I would say the value of the real option is about ten grand and Gus is getting a bargain by offering about half of that."

"So you think I should reject his offer and ask for a figure closer to the ten thousand?" Alice asked.

"That is a better price of what the option is worth. But this opens up a whole other set of questions. Who is Gus Kunz and how did he come up with a price that exactly what Ophelia was offering? Why does he show up here so soon after Ophelia's death? "

"It is curious," Alice puzzled.

"I think it is more than curious," Hannah intoned.

"Will you do something for me? When Gus calls again, tell him the price of the option is $15 thousand."

"That is much more than the $10 thousand you just calculated," Alice protested.

"I agree, but I want to see what his reaction is. How serious is he in wanting to acquire this shop and does he have information we don't?"

Closing the Deal

Hannah knocked on Nobel's back door and opened the door. "Nobel," she called.

"I'm in the den," Nobel responded.

As he came through the hallway he encountered Hannah followed by detective Hammersmith and Sergeant Rice. "What's up?" he asked.

"Alice called and said that Gus accepted her counter offer. He will pay the $15 grand. I then called the detective to tell him what we know."

As they sat in the living room, Hannah went over all that had happened. Then Nobel jumped in. "If Hannah didn't follow up on that hunch when she saw the little shop next to the proposed extension, we wouldn't be this far. I think she deserves a great deal of credit. I think you had better follow up on Gus Kunz. He might very well be your man."

"That is very interesting," Hammersmith mused.

"You know he was never even on the radar," Rice added.

Later that week, Hammersmith reported that Gus was involved in a front organization that marketed in drugs behind the scenes from a chain of costume and theater supply shops across the country. He was having a difficult time getting a foothold in the local area and Alice's shop could have been a critical link. Ophelia just seemed have gotten in the way.

Once the lead was identified the police were able to take the case to a satisfactory conclusion.

Summary of Concepts

Real Options

"Real options valuation, also often termed real options analysis[14], (ROV or ROA) applies option valuation techniques to capital budgeting decisions[15]. A real option itself, is the right — but not the obligation — to undertake certain business initiatives, such as deferring, abandoning, expanding, staging, or contracting a capital investment project. For example, the opportunity to invest in the expansion of a firm's factory, or alternatively to sell the factory, is a real call or put option, respectively. Real options are generally distinguished from conventional financial options in that they are not typically traded as securities, and do not usually involve decisions on an underlying asset that is traded as a financial security[16]"

Expected NPV

In this case the expected NPV is the weighted average of the upside NPV and the downside NPV.

Maximized NPV

The maximized NPV is calculated by taking the best NPV from two alternatives for any branch on a decision tree times the probability that branch occurring. Suppose the two branches are upside (best case) and downside (worst case) and each branch have a choice of either going forward or not. The two branches must be options based on an external event that is uncontrollable by the

---

[14] http://ardent.mit.edu/real_options/RO_current_lectures/borison.pdf
[15] https://faculty.fuqua.duke.edu/~charvey/Teaching/BA456 2002/Identifying_real_options.htm
[16] http://www.csn.ul.ie/~karen/Articles/Real%20Options.pdf

257

decision maker. By waiting the decision maker can obtain better information and then decide to do it or not. If the downside is a negative outcome then the decision maker would not go forward and would reduce the loss by not going forward. This minimization of loss results in the overall expected NPV being maximized.

GBER

Learning Objectives

An understanding of:
Working Capital Management
Net Operating Profit After Taxes (NOPAT)
Invested Capital
Weighted Average Cost of Capital (WACC)
Fixed and Variable Costs
Break-Even Analysis
Global Break-Even Revenue

Spreadsheet Tools found at
www.businessallstars.com/calculator

Assessment found at
www.businessallstars.com/assessment

A Flight to Paris

Noble Merchant walked slowly toward the boarding area and glanced at his watch. He still had time before the first call to board. He spotted a free seat a few rows away in the morass of waiting passengers lounging in the connected chairs and worked his way to it. He sat down, placed his carry-on between his feet and fumbled with the book he had just purchased at the gift shop and the leather bound zippered loose-leaf.

Taking a deep breath he glanced out the window to see if his plane was at the gate and as he did caught sight of a smartly dressed woman seated a few seats down and across from him. She was obviously a confident woman of some means.

Returning his focus to his book, he overheard the attendant announce that first class passengers were boarding. He stood, gathered his things and began to make his way toward the gate. He produced his ticket, had it scanned and proceeded toward the door. Once inside the plane he found his seat number, stowed his bag in the overhead compartment and sat down. As he did, the woman he had noticed in the terminal was suddenly standing to his side reaching up and placing a bag in the overhead compartment next to his.

"Excuse me; I think that is my seat, by the window," she motioned across him.

He stood up, slid to the side, and let her pass---to the seat next to his. Being a people watcher at heart, his attention was drawn away from the woman and to the boarding passengers. They filed in one after another, passed him and were lost somewhere behind him in the plane. He couldn't help feeling thankful that he was in first class where he had a little leg room and not cocooned surrounded by restrictive barriers on all sides.

Eventually, the attendant closed the door and everyone began to settle in.

The plane made a smooth take-off, gained altitude and then leveled off. As it did he inspected his book: front cover, back cover, title page, and introduction--- everything. Then he went to page one and began to lose himself in the journey the book offered. He paid little attention to the woman in the seat next to him until he became aware that she seemed to be looking at the loose-leaf that was resting on his lap. As he turned in her direction, she glanced up and then away to the window. He looked down to see the bold lettering emblazoned on the cover of his loose-leaf: "What's Your GBER."

Noble didn't know whether to say anything or not. It was always a question. Do you open the door of conversation with the passenger in the next seat and risk being bluntly put off and then suffering a awkward social situation for the next several hours? On the other hand, his business was GBER and this seemed to be a natural lead in. The next time she glanced around, he spoke up: "Hello, are you going to Paris on business?" It was a lame question, but it began the conversation.

"Yes, are you?"

"As a matter of fact I am. I'm presenting a training session to a few European executives on the value of GBER."

"I noticed your leading line---'What's Your GBER. It sounds interesting."

"It is meant to get people's attention."

"Do I dare ask what a GBER is?" she queried somewhat reluctantly.

"Before I answer that, do you mind if I ask you a few questions?"

"You can try," she replied guardedly.

"What kind of business are you in?"

"I own a boutique that sells up-market specialized women's apparel."

"How is business?"

"We have been open for about three years and I'm proud to say we are in the black."

"That's great. Is this a buying trip?"

"Are you sure you're not with the IRS?"

"I promise. It is just that I like to assess the frame of reference relative to our common interest in business. GBER is a global metric that tells me how your business is really doing."

"What do you mean by 'really doing'? I told you I'm in the black, covering all my costs and making a little extra."

"How much background do you have in financial analysis?"

"I emphasized marketing in college, if that's what you're wondering."

"I would assume you had to take basic courses in economics, accounting and finance as a part of your degree program?"

"There were a few along the way. I did pretty well in them, but probably couldn't tell you much of anything that was covered."

"I see: a classic case of bulimic learning. You fattened up during the course and then purged on the final."

She shrugged her shoulders. "Hey, I'm a marketing person, and now a small business owner who has a major debt and tons of optimism."

"Perhaps you shouldn't show me your GBER. I would hate to take the wind out of your sails," he offered reluctantly.

"Now you do have my interest. How can GBER compromise my enthusiasm?"

"Oh, it wouldn't, but it might give you a different perspective." He normally charged clients a major fee for continuing past this point, but she was very interesting to him on many levels. "Do you drive a car?"

"Yes."

"GBER is not the car, the road, the driver, or the journey. It is much like the speedometer that can tell you critical data about your driving experience, but only if you choose to employ it. Some people think financial analysis is a magical tool that can cure what ails the business. It simply gives you information. The rest is up to you. It's much like college: it gives you tools, a degree, and even access to employment, but once on the job, the actual performance is what you make of it."

"Got it," she snapped.

"Let me see if you recall any financial terms from your undergraduate program. Do you remember NOPAT, WACC, Invested Capital, Break-Even Analysis, Excess Earnings, Residual Income, or EVA?" he queried.

"Only vaguely, but remember, I was a marketing major."

"Yes, but now you are a business owner."

"True," she confessed. "Go on."

"To do this right, I would need to know a lot more about your business---financially."

She hesitated and he could tell she was weighing the benefit versus cost of sharing more intimate details of her business. Finally, she said, "I was about to review my past year's performance during the flight. I have a set of financials here in my carry-on." She motioned to an executive bag at her feet. She reached down, opened her bag and pulled a folder from it. As she did, he raised his tray from its hiding place and secured it in front of him as his working table.

She held the folder in her hand, studied him for a long moment and then sat it on his tray. He wondered to himself if this was the first step toward---surrendering to him. There seemed to be a personal connection between them that he did not understand, and couldn't help but wonder if she felt it too.

An Intimate Portrait

He opened the folder and peered at the data. "This is quite an operation. You had total revenue of about $5 million last year, cost of goods sold of $2 million and a bottom line of a hundred thousand. Not bad, that is about a two percent net income." He flipped through the supporting pages. "It looks like you have quarterly data here also. Are these numbers on a cash or accrual basis?"

"I think my accountant said he converts them to quasi-accrual at the end of each reporting period--- whatever that means."

"A lot of smaller companies record transactions as they pay or receive cash. Like a check book. These cash flows can swing wildly from one quarter to the next, depending on how people feel about the cash both coming and going. This can result in some quarters looking absolutely wonderful and others a disaster. Accrual accounting helps to smooth things out and reflect a matching of revenues earned and the expenses that generated those revenues. It is a better way. I'm glad your accountant does this for you."

"He seems pretty thorough," she admitted.

"Well, the first step is to convert Net Income into 'Net Operating Profit After Taxes' or what is commonly called NOPAT. Normally, to do a full blown analysis we would make several adjustments, but for our purposes we will do a quick and dirty."

"Why do we want NOPAT as you call it?"

"There are several expenses that are subtracted before we calculate Net Income that are not a part of NOPAT. One of these is interest expense. It is subtracted from Revenue as an operating cost when in fact it is a financing cost."

"What's the difference?"

"When you started your business did you have to buy a lot of stuff? You know, I mean hard assets."

"Yes, I had to have my location remodeled to my specifications. Talk about a conversion, I had to transform a failed toy store into a very exclusive women's boutique that sold high end clothing. That was not easy. In addition to moving walls, painting, electrical and plumbing I had to purchase specialized fixtures, furniture."

"So you invested in assets that should last for several years before they need to be replaced?"

"That's right," she agreed as she reached over, shuffled through the papers and pointed out the property, plant and equipment under the heading fixed assets listed on the balance sheet. "There, it cost me close to a million dollars to get started."

"Part came from my personal assets, part from family, and the rest from a small business loan. I put up the original half million, but I've had to go to my family for an additional $200,000 to cover what my accountant calls working capital."

"I'm sure the interest expense or financial cost is related to that loan?" he offered.

"That's right," she countered.

"I'm going to jot down some of your numbers on this yellow pad so I can do some figuring. I'll only show the numbers in thousands, which means I'll drop the three digits at the end of each number just for ease in working with them (Figure 9-1)."

Figure 9-1

Balance Sheet (Year end)		Portrait
Cash & Cash Equivalents	150	
Accounts Receivable	325	OA
Inventory	300	
Other Current Assets	150	
Current Assets	925	
Property, Plant & Equip	1,000	IA
Accumulated Deprec	(375)	
Total Assets	1,550	
Accounts Payable	250	OA
Other Current Liabilities	50	
Current Liabilities	300	
Notes Payable	500	
Total Debt	800	FA
Common Stock	700	
Retained Earnings	50	
Total Liab & Equity	1,550	

"There," he said with pride as he copied the balance sheet and created a document he could make notes on. "If I were an artist I couldn't have sketched a better picture of you, but not just a portrait in a studio. This is a picture that shows your physical appearance and your character as well. It tells me your strengths and weaknesses, your ability to keep your commitments, and who can exercise power over you. It tells me your age, if you trust other people and if they trust you. I know more

267

about you by looking at this statement than if I were to see you naked in your bath."

"You think so, do you?" she said with skepticism and a smirk. "What do you think, am I decent or not?"

"You look pretty good, not great, but pretty good." He could sense that her physical beauty, the way she carried herself and the clothing she wore intimidated most people. Perhaps she found it refreshing to find someone who didn't acquiesce to her powers or maybe she saw him as a challenge yet to be conquered. Of course he was interested in her and flattered that she would trust him enough to share the numbers, but he had no intention of giving her the upper hand.

"Tell me, who has power over me?" she asked. She did not even flinch concerning the naked comment, but the issue of control obviously touched a nerve.

I Believe in You

"On the asset side you have $325,000 of uncollected accounts receivable. These are customers that have power because they did not pay in cash, but demanded credit and you gave it to them. As a matter of fact, if I divide your $5,000,000 annual revenue by 365 days, you generate about $13,700 per day in sales."

Sales per day
$5,000,000 / 365 = $13,700

"If I divide the $325,000 in accounts receivable by your sales per day, we just calculated, you have about 24 days of sales that are uncollected at any one time. Putting it another way, it takes you a little over three and a half weeks to collect after a sale is made."

Accounts Receivable days
$325,000 / $13,700 = 24 days

"Do you think that's good or bad?"

"It seems high to me for a retail shop where most people pay with a credit card, which is almost like cash. I think you have some very high end women that like to carry an account with you."

"That's exactly how it is. I remember the day the president of the women's guild came in. She wanted to purchase a stunning blue ensemble I brought back from Milan. It wasn't even a question of whether or not she could afford it. She wanted to set up a revolving account and charge it. I saw this as a way to capture even more of her business and establish a permanent customer. It was one of the best decisions I ever made, because it led to an explosion of business from the women's guild."

"I would suspect you have very few accounts that are uncollected and have to be written off?"

"There are a few, but not many. We are very selective and our clients know it. This wasn't a way of surrendering power, but rather of forming a partnership with the powerful."

The Discount Shop

"You also have $300,000 in inventory which must be sold in the near future. If I check the numbers and divide $2,000,000 Cost of Goods Sold by 365 days, I calculate that sales cost you about $5,500 per day."

$$\textit{Cost of Goods Sold per day}$$
$$\$2,000,000 / 365 = \$5,500$$

"Dividing the $300,000 inventory by the $5,500 in the cost of daily sales indicates that an item will remain on the racks for almost 55 days before it goes out the door. That is nearly two months. I'm not a retail expert and certainly not when it comes to women's fashion, but is that reasonable?"

$$\textit{Inventory days}$$
$$\$300,000 / \$5,500 = 55 \text{ days}$$

"I never calculated that number, but have a general sense that is correct," she confirmed.

"Once again your customers have the power to make or break you. If they buy, you move inventory and it's not a problem. If they don't, you will have to slash prices or even write some things off. I would say your customers have a significant amount of power over you."

"You make it sound as though my customers are tyrants and I'm their slave. I have a great reputation and most of my customers feel it is a real privilege to purchase something from my shop. I'm not so sure I agree with your assessment."

"I would suspect one of the most critical aspects of your business is the buying trip."

"You're absolutely right. I'm the shop and the shop is me. What I buy is what we sell and my clients count on my judgment and expertise. I don't have a lot of ability with the figures in financial statements, but I have tremendous talent in knowing what to put on the figures of my clients."

"What becomes of clothing that does not sell? Do you have some process for dealing with older items that remain on the racks?"

"Because we don't sell in bulk and most of our pieces are unique I don't feel compelled to move them out if they don't sell in the requisite time frame. If an item remains on the racks longer than I think it should, I must make a decision. I've only recently set up a separate shop where I offer items at prices below full retail. That has been a gamble for me, because I don't want to compromise my brand and send the wrong message. It is a bare bones rented space about a block from my main location."

She continued, "It is amazing to see how many women want to wear high-end apparel on a budget. It is opening up a whole new market where I'm beginning to buy items that go straight to that shop. I really feel that I'm controlling that market, it is not controlling me." She paused and then added, "Is that all you've got?"

Power Trio

"No, there's more. The two operating assets we just discussed, accounts receivable and inventory, plus one of your operating liabilities, accounts payable, I refer

to as the power trio (Figure 9-2). They provide the
financial power to your business; the operating energy, so
to speak."

Figure 9-2

Cash & Cash Equivalents	150	
Accounts Receivable	325	OA
Inventory	300	
Other Current Assets	150	
Current Assets	925	

Accounts Payable	250	
Other Current Liabilities	50	OA
Current Liabilities	300	

He pointed to a spot further down on the balance
sheet. "You have $250,000 of outstanding accounts
payable. This represents claims on your business by
vendors who have extended credit to you when you
purchased inventory from them. I divided accounts
receivable by revenue per day because those numbers
were both at cost plus mark-up. I use cost of goods sold
per day when analyzing inventory and accounts payable
because they are carried at cost, without any mark-up
added."

"We just calculated the cost of goods sold per day
as $5,500. If I divide that number into the $250,000 of
accounts payable it tells me that from the time you
receive your goods it takes you about 45 days to pay the
vendors."

Account Payable days
$250,000 / $5,500 = 45 days

"That is a month and a half. Until you pay the bills these vendors have a direct claim on your business. It does show they have great faith in you, but if they ever decided to stop extending credit, you would be in a world of hurt."

"Everything you have mentioned so far, I'm totally aware of. You see, because credit is given and received it is not that they have power over me; it is more a validation of my superior ability to run a business. They want to move product and they trust me. The fact that I can extend payment to 45 days is more a measure of the power I have and not the other way around."

"I like your optimism."

"You don't succeed in business without confidence and faith in yourself," She noted.

"It takes 55 days to sell an item and another 24 days to collect from the customer. That is a total of 79 days from the time you receive your inventory, sell it and then collect from the customer. You have to finance all those days of current assets."

Current Asset days
55 days + 24 days = 79 days

"One way to finance the build-up in inventory and receivables is to delay the payment of your payables. By paying in 45 days, your vendors (suppliers) are financing part of your current assets. The net credit days is 79 days minus 45 days or 34 days that you are exposed."

Net Credit days
79 days − 45 days = 34 days

"You need to find additional outside financing to pay for those 34 days of credit. That is why your

accountant said you needed the additional investment,"
he noted.

She paused a moment. "Anyone else you think
has power over me?"

He had the sense their discussion was turning into
a duel or a fencing match at thirty thousand feet in the air.
He would attack and she would defend and then counter
attack. She seemed to enjoy the challenge, and besides,
all the attention was on her and she appeared to love it.

The Gamblers

His finger moved to the bottom of the page:

Figure 9-3

Notes Payable	500	
Total Debt	800	FA
Common Stock	700	
Retained Earnings	50	

"Two other areas: You have Notes Payable of $500,000. The $200,000 of the Common Stock that was invested by people, other than yourself and your original $500,000 are part of the $700,000 shown on the balance sheet (Figure 9-3). The Notes Payable bunch---they demand interest and principle on a very rigid schedule and if those payments are missed, you are out of business. Those who invested in your company are willing to risk receiving nothing in return."

"Let me just say there is a lot of history behind those numbers. You can't imagine what I had to go through to get that loan. The money from my family--- that is a completely different story," she said.

Borrowed Money

"Before I ever opened my boutique, I had been planning that event for years. In high school, a local department store selected a group of girls from my school to be on a special fashion board. I was one of those chosen and worked closely with buyers at the store. I'll never forget our discussions about fabrics, colors, trends, and markets. I was hooked.

"That year, for my prom dress, I personally selected this incredible dark blue number from the store and felt like an absolute knock-out at the dance. I wanted every other girl to have the same thrill that I experienced.

"After high school, I worked my way through college part time for the store, in the backroom stocking all the goods, then as an assistant on the floor during evenings and weekends and finally, as a full commission sales associate in my senior year.

"After college I went to New York and enrolled in a graduate program in fashion merchandising. I never finished the program because I landed a job at an exclusive boutique. From that point on, I worked my tail off and saved every dime I could with the idea that someday I would have my own shop.

"I realized that I had an eye, or what you might call a gift, for picking what really sold and matched current trends. I was an information bloodhound, reading every fashion magazine, association and trade publication, and article from any source that related to the industry and trends. At first I would travel with the main buyer and assist on selections. The items I chose were almost always the best movers at the store. Eventually, I was made the lead buyer for some of the markets.

"When I finally could scrounge half a million from all savings, personal resources, credit cards, a second mortgage and whatever, I decided to go out on my own. That is when the fun began.

"I looked at various other sources of financing, and what an education that was. I had to go through a checklist like you can't believe. Well, you probably can. My business plan had to address the business purpose, mission, strategy, markets, products, pricing, competition, suppliers, trademarks and brands."

"They wanted to know all about my background: what skills and abilities I would bring to the table. They wanted to know who else was involved and what their backgrounds were, had worked together before and what was the organizational structure. That was all before we got into the numbers.

"My accountant helped me with an estimate of what funds we would need and how they would be used. We had to forecast revenues for the next five years and a detailed cash flow projection, by month for the first three years. It was amazing."

He interjected. "I don't think that is unusual. They are gambling their money on you."

"I looked at all the various sources of financing. Venture Capitalists wanted over 50% control of the business and a 75% return each year. Then they would sell off the business after three to five years. I found an Angel Investor, but they wanted 25 and 25: twenty-five percent equity ownership and a 25% return each year. Finally, a bank agreed to a loan through the Small Business Administration. No equity ownership was involved, but a very strict repayment plan was required.

"After I put up my money and the banks money I launched the business. That is when I found out how to rapidly expand the business by extending credit to the women from the guild. It was going to take even more money, but I was tapped out.

Other Equity

"Someone told me another option was FFF or Family, Friends, and Fools. I have a rich Uncle Walter who I thought might help. When I talked to him it was probably one of the most depressing moments in my family history. He flatly said no."

"When I got home that night I got a call from Aunt Jenny, Walter's wife. She was not there when I talked with Uncle Walter, but when she heard about what I wanted she pretty well told Walter where to put it. Now,

I always thought I was Walter's favorite and Jenny was a little distant, but you can never tell. She told me to come back the next day and she would have a check waiting with no strings attached. Wow!"

"I look at these sources of financing not as an extension of power over me, but as a validation of who I am." Then pointing to the page she asked, "What are these things on the side---OA, IA, and FA?"

"Accountants like to groups of items on the balance sheet as Operating, Investing, or Financing Activity. It is just too bad that financial analysts haven't caught up to this. It would be a lot easier if the two fields were more integrated."

"Let's move on to the Income Statement," he said.

Not Your Dad's Net Income

"The decision regarding how much to borrow, is completely independent from the ongoing operations of the business. If you financed the whole business from your own savings, there would be no debt and no interest expense. If you borrowed the whole amount, then the interest expense would be much larger. The point being: financing decisions are generally very different from ongoing operating decisions---salaries, rent, utilities, insurance, supplies, advertising, and such."

"Okay."

She leaned in close to look at the numbers and he took a deep breath, savoring a gentle fragrance that seemed to surround her. As he paused she sensed the delay and leaned back expecting him to continue the explanation.

He looked down at the pages, turned back to the income statement and pointed to the interest expense. "If we subtract the $60,000 of interest expense from the other expenses then the bottom line will increase by that amount. But not only that: If we didn't have the interest expense, then income taxes would be much higher. We say that interest expense provides a tax break."

"That's good isn't it?"

"Sure, but it also means that your true cost for interest expense is not the $60,000. Let me see." He quickly crunched some numbers in his head. "Taxes were $33,000, so if I add that back to the Net Income of $100,000, the before tax amount would be $133,000."

Before Tax Income
$100,000 + $33,000 = $133,000

"It looks like the tax rate was about 25%, or $33,000 taxes on $133,000 of before-tax income."

Income Tax Rate
$33,000 / $133,000 = 25%

"If I increase the before-tax amount by the interest expense that is no longer a part of the income statement, then it will be $133,000 plus $60,000 or $193,000."

Before Tax Income excluding Interest Expense
$133,000 + $60,000 = $193,000

"Twenty-five percent tax on that amount would be about $48,000, so you get a $15,000 tax break because of having interest expense."

Adjusted Income Tax Amount
$193,000 x 25% = $48,000

Tax Break because of no Interest Expense
$48,000 - $33,000 = $15,000

"If you take out the interest expense, which increases the before tax amount and apply the same tax rate to the new total? Then, $193,000 minus $48,000 would leave $145,000."

Net Operating Profit After Taxes
$193,000 - $48,000 = $145,000

She shook her head, "You lost me."

Figure 9-4

Before			After
Revenue	$5,000	$5,000	Revenue
Oper Exp	($4,682)	($4,682)	Oper Exp
Depr. Exp	($125)	($125)	Depr Exp
Int Exp	($60)		
Taxes	($33)	($48)	Taxes
Total Exp	($4,900)	($4,855)	Oper. Exp
Net Inc	$100	$145	NOPAT

He pointed to the figures on his sheet (Figure 9-4). "Instead of $100,000 of Net Income, we now have $145,000 NOPAT or Net Operating Profit After-Taxes."

"So we just don't use interest expense and the related taxes at all?"

"We are going to use them, but later."

Just then the attendant came by offering some refreshment and the discussion about GBER was put on hold. They made small talk for a while as they ate. She had the appearance of someone very confident that could put you in your place very quickly, but there seemed to be some connection between them that made talking to her very exciting. All the signals that she sent were sincere, and so he went with it.

Suddenly, she turned to him and said, "So why do we want NOPAT?"

"We can't use Net Income because interest expense is incorporated into it, but we still need to know what our operating profit is. So we call our new number NOPAT."

"What comes next?"

281

"The next thing we need to do is find out what it costs you to finance your company."

"Well, that seems very simple. The interest expense is $60,000."

"That is the cost to finance the debt or what you borrowed. There is still the cost of equity." He opened the financial statements to the balance sheet and pointed to the liabilities and equity. "Some of these liabilities have no cost associated with them: such as Accounts Payable and Other Accruals. So if we subtract those from the total, everything that is left has a cost."

She looked at the numbers. "There is the half a million I borrowed and the rest of the stuff is what my family and I put up, plus some profits my accountant calls retained earnings."

Figure 9-5

Notes Payable	500	
Total Debt	800	FA
Common Stock	700	
Retained Earnings	50	

"That's right, a half million in debt and the $750,000 in equity."

"But the equity doesn't cost me anything."

"On the contrary, it costs you a great deal, much more that the $60,000 interest expense on the half million. The interest cost is about 12%, excluding the tax benefit."

Before Tax Cost of Debt
$60,000 / $750,000 = 12%

"If I count that $15,000 in tax savings because of the interest expense, then the true cost is $45,000 divided by $500,000 or about 9%."

After Tax Cost of Debt
$45,000 / $750,000 = 9%

What's Your Salary

"Now I'm going to assume you pay yourself a pretty decent salary plus perks," he continued.

Suddenly, she became a little cooler. It appeared that the mention of her salary and perks were a sensitive issue.

He recovered quickly. "You don't need to tell me exactly what you earn, but I'm going to make some theoretical assumptions. Let's say you pay yourself about $400,000 a year."

Before she could say anything he interjected, "just go with me on this."

"Okay," she said skeptically.

"Suppose for some reason you could not work directly at the boutique, what would you pay a manager to come in and handle things?"

"Well, assuming I was taking $400,000 per year. You know I not only manage the place, I do all the buying and am basically responsible for everything."

"What if you hired a manager to run the day-to-day and another person to do the buying, what would you pay them?"

"I might pay them $100,000 each," she concluded.

"That's $200,000 compared to the $400,000 you are taking. The difference of $200,000 is really a dividend or a return on your equity investment as an owner."

Dividend (Excess Salary to Owner/Manager)
$400,000 - $200,000 = $200,000

"Are you saying the salaries expense on my income statement is wrong? That it is overstated by $200,000?"

"Not exactly, I'm just saying your salary as the owner has two parts. One part is the payment for your management ability and buying expertise. The other part is compensation for being the owner that you would not normally pay to hired employees."

"This is much like the interest expense. It is financing cost embedded in the operating expenses of the company, but instead of cost paid to those who lent you money, it goes to those who invested in the equity. It also needs to be adjusted for taxes. The taxes on $200,000 would be $50,000 or 25% of it. We subtract that to end up with a net cost to the business of $150,000. "

Taxes on Dividend
$200,000 x 25% = $50,000

After Tax Dividend
$200,000 - $50,000 = $150,000

She clarified, "What you're saying is the $150,000 after-tax excessive salary that I received is a return on my equity investment and is a financing cost to the company, not an operating cost. But it does nothing for Aunt Jenny and Uncle Walter."

"That is right. Technically they should be receiving a return on their investment. Because they did not receive a dividend they will have to see their return in the form of the growth in the value of their investment."

284

We will adjust the Income Statement once more by subtracting your dividend from Operating Expenses and raising the Taxes Expense by another $50,000 (Figure 9-6).

Figure 9-6

	Before	After	
Revenue	$5,000	$5,000	Revenue
Oper Exp	($4,682)	($4,482)	Oper Exp
Depr. Exp	($125)	($125)	Depr Exp
Int Exp	($60)		
Taxes	($33)	($98)	Taxes
Total Exp	($4,900)	($4,705)	Oper. Exp
Net Inc	$100	$295	NOPAT

"If we look at the newly adjusted NOPAT of $295,000 we find three things there: $100,000 of original Net Income, $150,000 of net dividends to equity holders and $45,000 of net interest expense. The net income of $100,000 belongs to the equity investors but instead of being paid out to them is invested back into the company. The next $150,000 was paid out as dividend to some equity investors and the $45,000 was paid as net interest expense to those who lent you money."

Reconciling Net Income to NOPAT
$100,000 + $150,000 + $45,000 = $295,000

"The company had investing activity when it purchased Fixed Assets. I'm going to introduce a new

285

term that I call Invested Capital. It represents the total cash investment that shareholders and debt-holders have made in a company. There are two different but completely equivalent methods for calculating invested capital."

"The *operating approach* is calculated as: Invested capital = operating current assets – operating current liabilities + net property, plant & equipment + capitalized operating leases + other operating assets + operating intangibles – other operating liabilities – cumulative adjustment for amortization of R&D."

"The *financing approach* is calculated as: Invested capital = total debt and leases + total equity and equity equivalents – non-operating cash and investments.[1]"

"It sounds pretty complex, but let's calculate your Invested Capital under either approach (Figure 9-7).

Figure 9-7

Operating Approach		Financing Approach	
Oper C/A	$925	$500	N/Pay
Oper C/L	($300)	$200	C/S FFF
P, P & E	$1,000	$500	C/S Own
Acc Depr	($375)	$50	Ret Earn
Inv Cap	$1,250	$1,250	Inv Cap

"If I look at the Financing Approach I see there are four sources of financing. We need to determine what percent each of the sources of financing represents for the foreseeable future and the cost for each. If we divide each

[17] http://en.wikipedia.org/wiki/Invested_capital

amount by the total we can see its weight as a percent of the total. For example $500 is 40% of the total."

<u>Debt Weight Calculation</u>
$500 / $1,250 = 40%

"We can do the same for each of the others and find the weights for each. (Figure (9-8)"

"We already said that the true after-tax cost of debt for the company was 9%. Let me ask you a question. How much do you expect the company to grow each of the next few years?" Noble asked.

"We are doing really well. I would say we could continue to grow by 20% for each of the next five years at least."

Figure 9-8

	Amount	Weight
Debt	$500	40.0%
C/S FFF	$200	16.0%
C/S Own	$500	40.0%
Ret Earn	$50	4.0%
Fin Cap	$1,250	

"Given that your relatives are not expecting any dividend they will participate in a return by seeing the value of their investment grow by the 20%. That seems pretty reasonable. I'm going to group the retained earnings with your own common stock amount and say the third category represents 44% of the total. We need to determine the cost to the company of that portion. If the net dividend paid by the company was $150,000 on an investment of $550,000 then the dividend yield would be 27.3%."

Dividend Yield

$150,000 / $550,000 = 27.3%

"But that is not the only return you expect. We need to add the 20% growth expectation to that to get the full cost."

Dividend Yield

27.3% + 20.0% = 47.3%

"Wow, I guess I never expected to put it into those types of terms," she mused.

"We should normally project this over a long time frame, but my quick and dirty approach has given us a number that is probably in the ball park."

"You are beginning to know a lot more about me personally than I expected. Are you sure GBER isn't a term for something we shouldn't be discussing as almost total strangers?"

"It is nothing of a personally intimate nature, but my intent is to completely undress your company and get to the real figures."

She studied him for a long moment and then said, "I can handle it. Where do we go from here?"

Take a Whack at That

"We need to combine the various parts of financing cost into a single measure we will call the Weighted Average Cost of Capital. Remember we said the debt costs 9% after taxes, the FFF expectation is around 20% and your own is 47.3%."

"Yes."

"If we multiply the weight of debt times the after-tax cost of debt we get a component cost of 3.6%."

Component Cost of Debt
40% x 9% = 3.6%

"Then if we multiply the weight of FFF equity times the cost of equity we get a component cost of 3.2%."

Component Cost of FFF Equity
16% x 20% = 3.2%

"Lastly, if we multiply the weight of your own equity times its cost of equity we get a component cost of 3.2%."

Component Cost of Own Equity
44% x 47.3% = 20.8%

"Adding these three components together we get a weighted average cost of 27.6%."

Weighted Average Cost of Capital
3.6% + 3.2% + 20.8% = 27.6%

"That is what it costs your company for the financing it maintains."

Figure 9-9

	Weight	Cost	component
Debt	40.0%	9%	3.6%
C/S FFF	16.0%	20.0%	3.2%
C/S Own	44.0%	47.3%	20.8%
Fin Cap	100%		27.6%

"Why do I want to know that?" she wondered.

"Every company needs financing to operate and for expansion. It is critical the company understand what the cost of their combined financing is when it comes to evaluating operating and growth decisions. If the return you generate from operating the business is not greater than the cost to finance the operations, then you should rethink the decision. It offers a hurdle or required return for most decisions."

"There is something about you I find very intriguing. I'm totally aware of the people around me and when you first checked me out at the terminal, my initial impression was that you were very interesting. Then when I found that we were seated next to each other I was hoping you would attempt to talk with me. Do you know what it was about you that intrigued me?"

Taken aback, he wondered what was coming next.

"It was your eyes and that stupid title: 'Show Me Your GBER.' The more we've talked, the more I've gained respect for your intellect. Now don't take this wrong, but most people in my world are extremely superficial and caught up in outward appearances. That's

290

just the world I work in. You are surprisingly deep and refreshing, in a number-crunching kind of way."

"I don't quite know what to say." He was taken aback by the direct evaluation. "Where do we go from here?"

"You finish telling about this GBER thing, and what I'm trying to say is that I like you."

He took a deep breath. His mind was racing. He really didn't care what she thought of him, he had enough confidence to take whatever she said with a grain of salt. He had correctly assessed her to begin with. She was a power woman with a great figure and clothes to match, but damn it, he liked her too. "Okay, let us recap. What is NOPAT?"

"It is the Net Operating Profit for the year, excluding interest expense, hidden dividends to owners and the related tax savings for each."

"How much is yours?"

"It is $295,000."

"Excellent. What is Financing Capital?"

"It is the moneys lent to the company or invested in the company that have an associated cost."

"How much is yours?"

She looked through her notes. "It is $1,250,000."

"What is the cost of debt?" he continued.

"It is interest expense less the tax savings divided by the debt outstanding."

"And your cost is?"

"My cost of debt is 9%," she said with pride.

"Good. What is the cost of equity?"

"It has two parts. The cost of equity from Family, Friends, and Fools is 20% and the cost of equity from my own investment is 47.3%.

"What is the WACC?"

"It is the weighted average cost of financing the company."

"What is your WACC?"

"Once again, based on your theoretical numbers, it would be 27.6%."

"Wow."

She smiled with great pride and looked absolutely amazing. Her eyes seemed to sparkle and he was afraid that his did also. The attendant was back again with another service and so they took another break from the numbers. "I have a proposal," he said.

"What is that?" she responded with one eyebrow raised.

"I don't know your name, where you are from, if you are married or otherwise involved. I don't even really know where you are going other than a purchasing trip with a flight landing in Paris. Let's assume that none of that matters. We will share this flight and this discussion. We will enjoy this moment and never see each other again."

She wrinkled her brow at the strange suggestion and then after a quick reflection said, "That is a wonderful idea." He suspected that in the back of her mind it was her intent anyway, but he had actually put it into words.

He continued, "You see, with no potential for any follow-up or other connection, we can enjoy a bad blind date without regard to any baggage."

"Are you saying I would be a bad blind-date?"

"Not at all, I just remember a girl much like you who was physically attractive and very popular who ended up as my date in high school. I knew that she wondered how she ever got stuck with me. She did not have the capability to celebrate an evening with someone very different from herself, explore the adventure of a unique opportunity and leave it at that."

She seemed to accept his explanation. After dinner most of the people around them were settling into the movie that was provided or just sleeping. "Are we getting any closer?" she asked.

"I still think Paris is several hours away."

"No, I was referring to the illusive GBER"

"Oh. Well, the next thing we need to do is investigate Break-Even Analysis," he instructed.

"I'm ready," she offered with encouragement.

A Little Short

"Most companies use Break-Even analysis to look at the operations of a department or operating unit. I think it can be used for a more global view. The problem with classical Break-Even is that it ends up determining how many units should be produced so the revenues exactly equal the expenses. In that case the units have to be homogeneous or all the same. Things get really muddy when a department has multiple types of products at varying costs or prices."

"That sounds relatively restrictive. I have one store, and it has various departments, but even in each department we sell so many different priced goods that it sounds as if Break-Even has no applicability."

"I have determined the easiest way to equate everything on a relative scale is to talk in terms of price and total revenue instead of total units. So I try to determine the revenue that would be required to Break-Even and not the number of units."

"Will total revenue take care of all the differences?" she questions.

"Not all of them and it is still somewhat imperfect, but it is the best for a quick analysis."

"I can accept that, but you know---it doesn't cost me any more to sell a very expensive item than an inexpensive one. As a result, I would think mix becomes a fairly critical thing."

"You are jumping ahead of me, but that is good, it just shows that you are becoming invested in the analysis."

"Well, this is my business, and my life," she admitted.

"The next thing we need to focus on is costs. Do you remember the income statement we summarized (Figure 9-10)?

Figure 9-10

	Before		After	
Revenue	$5,000	$5,000	Revenue
Oper Exp	($4,682)	($4,482)	Oper Exp
Depr. Exp	($125)	($125)	Depr Exp
Int Exp	($60)		
Taxes	($33)	($98)	Taxes
Total Exp	($4,900)	($4,705)	Oper. Exp
Net Inc	$100	$295	NOPAT

"I have consolidated all other operating costs into the 'Operating Expenses' category except for depreciation, interest, and taxes. We need to break these Operating Expenses out into their fixed and variable components."

"What do you mean fixed and variable?"

Body and Clothing
He continued, "Bear with me for a moment here. I thought I saw some quarterly statements in your folder." He flipped through the pages. "Here they are. I'm going to summarize only the quarterly numbers for revenue and operating expenses for each quarter." He listed on a paper the following (Figure 9-11):

Figure 9-11

	1st Q	2nd Q	3rd Q	4th Q
Revenue	800	1,200	1,300	1,700
Oper Exp	900	1,050	1,180	1,352

"The Operating Expense excludes the excess salaries, depreciation expense, interest expense and taxes. If I add it up it will total $4,482, which agrees with our NOPAT statements. It appears that your sales are increasing and somewhat seasonal."

"That's right. Our biggest quarter is always the fourth quarter and our weakest is the first. Even at that we are seeing continued growth in sales, year over year. I'm still wondering about this fixed versus variable," she added.

"Over a short period which we call the relevant range, some of your costs will remain the same irrespective of the level of sales. Other costs will go up and down as revenue moves up or down. Over a short period of time we try to find how much will fit into either category. Over a longer period of time, say several years, you may convert some of the fixed to variable and some of the variable to fixed costs."

"What do you mean?"

"Let's talk about salaries. Fixed costs would be anyone who is paid a fixed monthly salary regardless of the level of sales. Variable costs would be commissions that are paid as a direct result of the level of sales. These are pure examples. There could also be salaries for some people that are mixed and have some fixed and variable elements."

"It sounds like a difficult problem trying to separate the two."

"It certainly can be. If you were to look at your list of operating costs and expenses: cost-of-goods-sold; salaries and wages; employee benefits; rent; utilities; supplies; advertising; insurance; licenses; sales taxes; professional fees; and other, it could be an overwhelming task to estimate how much of each was fixed and how much was variable."

"Absolutely," she admitted.

"There are easier ways to do this. Now that we have some data over time, such as the quarterly consolidated operating revenue and expense numbers, we can simply feed them into a program that can automatically calculate the fixed and variable for us. This will be pretty crude because for a statistical model like this to work with a fair degree of reliability we would need about thirty observations instead of just four. Even though this is pretty rough, it will give us some idea."

He unbuckled his seat belt, stood up in the aisle, opened the overhead compartment and began searching for his laptop. Once he found it he returned to his seat and turned it on: "I'm going to access a spreadsheet program and enter the quarterly numbers. Now I can highlight the data I want to analyze and ask the computer to graph the data with revenue across the bottom and expenses up the left hand side. Once these points are plotted I can ask the computer to fit a straight trend line through the points. The line may not go exactly through every point, but it does the best job it can. Then I ask the computer to give me a formula for the line and how well the data fits."

She leaned in close and studied what he was doing. Being a typical quantitative type he was more aware of the work he was doing than the closeness she offered. He highlighted the data that he wanted to use and clicked on an icon that translated the information into a graph. He then clicked on another menu item and a line appeared that ran through the four dots on the graph, followed by two formulas. The following image showed the results (Figure 9-12):

Figure 9-12

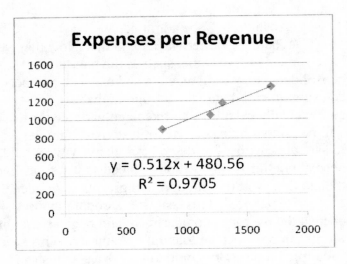

"Isn't that nice," he said with satisfaction.

"I recall something about this from a couple of my business courses, but it still makes very little sense."

"That's okay. You don't need to know everything about the process or how to even build it. What you do need to know is what it tells us."

"And what is that?"

"See the formula: $y = 0.512x + 480.56$?"

"Yes."

"The y is the operating expense level and the x is the revenue. As the revenue changes, it will dictate a specific expense level to match the sales. The 480.56 is the level of fixed costs per quarter. Regardless of the level of revenue there will be $480,560 in expenses every quarter over a relevant range. So from this you know that every quarter you will have at least that much in costs and expenses."

As he continued his explanation he noticed her long dark hair fall over his arm next to the computer. Was he being deceptive to enjoy the closeness of this beautiful creature under the pretext of explaining Break-Even?

"What does the 0.512 represent?" she asked.

"That is the variable cost piece. For every dollar in revenue you will incur 51.2 cents in costs. If you sell $1,000,000 in a month, you can expect variable costs to be 51.2% of that or $512,000. Theoretically, if in some quarter you sold nothing you would have zero variable costs but $480,560 in fixed costs and be losing money."

Total Cost with zero sales
(0.512 x 0) + $480,560 = $480,560

"On the other hand if you had revenue of $2,000,000 in a quarter you would have $480,560 in fixed costs and---let's see." He quickly multiplied $2,000,000 by .512. "And $1,024,000 in variable costs. Your total costs would be $1,494,561 and you would make money."

Total Cost with $2,000,000 sales
(0.512 x $2,000,000) + $480,560 = $1,024,000

"How does it help me to know this?" she wanted to know.

"If you are operating in the red, then you might want to consider converting some of your fixed costs to variable. If you are operating in the black it could be better to go the other direction and shift variable costs to fixed."

"How do I do that?"

"Some leases can be structured with more fixed than variable or more variable than fixed. Employees can be put on salary or straight commission. This can help management on both the downside and the upside."

"Interesting," she mused as she pulled back and studied him. "Okay, some costs are fixed and some are variable, where do we go from here?"

GBER

"Most educational programs that teach Break-Even use a model where fixed costs are divided by the contribution margin percentage to arrive at the required revenue."

"Wait a minute. What is contribution margin percentage? I don't recall talking about that."

"The contribution margin is the reciprocal or compliment of the variable cost factor. For every dollar of revenue you have 51.2 cents or 51.2 percent in variable costs. All the rest of the excess revenue contributes to paying for the fixed costs and any profit. In your case it would be $1.00 minus .512 or .488 cents."

<u>*Contribution Margin*</u>
100% - 51.2% = 48.8%

"This can also be stated in percentage terms as 48.8% of revenue goes to covering fixed costs and generating profit. Classical Break-Even probably includes all operating costs, depreciation, interest and excess salaries as fixed costs in the calculation. I have specifically excluded all three in this application."

"What about taxes?"

"Since we are talking about Break-Even there would be no taxes as the result of no profit."

"Okay," she agreed.

He explained, "When it comes to financing costs we must consider taxes because we will have to pay some to get to a point where there is no residual income. Invested Capital will be calculated by multiplying the WACC which was what?"

She quickly looked at the scribbling on the papers in front of them. "It is 27.6%."

"We multiply that percentage by the total Invested Capital which is?"

Once again she searched the numbers in front of them. "I can't find it."

"It is the total of Notes Payable and Equity on the Balance Sheet."

"That's right. It is $1,250,000."

"So, a WACC of 27.6% times total Invested Capital of $1,250,000 is $345,000. I call this the capital charge."

Capital Charge[18]
$1,250,000 fin. cap. x 27.6% WACC = $345,000

"Unfortunately, that is a before-tax number and so I need to know how much to earn before paying taxes."

"I thought you said there were no taxes in break-even," she complained.

"Technically, that is right, but when it comes to Invested Capital and WACC these are after-tax numbers and so a company would need to provide for taxes."

"Okay, if you say so," she conceded.

"To find the before tax amount we know that taxes represent 25% of the before tax number leaving 75% after taxes. Dividing the $345,000 by 75%, that it represents, we get $460,000 as the before tax number."

Before Tax Income (Break Even)
$345,000 / (1 - 25%) = $460,000

That is the amount that is added to all fixed operating costs. Do you recall what fixed operating costs were?"

---

[18] http://www.ventureline.com/accounting-glossary/C/capital-charge-definition/

She looked through the calculation again and said, "Here it is, $480,560."

"That was a quarterly number and so we need to multiply it by 4 to get the annual fixed cost," he explained.

Annual Fixed Cost
$480,560 x 4 = $1,922,240

"I also need to add $125,000 of depreciation expense as a fixed cost and so I get $2,047,240.

Annual Fixed Cost
$1,922,240 + $125,000 = $2,047,240

"I add $460,000, which is my grossed up capital charge to $2,047,240 and get $2,507,240 as my numerator."

Fixed Cost plus Before Tax Required Income
$2,047,240 + $480,560 = $2,507,240

"Dividing that number by my contribution margin percentage of 48.8%, gives me $5,137,787."

Global Break Even Revenue
$2,507,240 / 48.8% = $5,137,787

"And what is that?"

"That is your GBER."

"If I recast the financial statements showing the Global Break Even Revenue and the related Variable Costs, Contribution Margin, Fixed Costs, Depreciation Expense, EBIT, Taxes, NOPAT, and Capital Charge you can see that the residual income[19] is zero (figure 9-13)."

Figure 9-13

Global Break-Even Revenue

	Amount	%
Revenue	5,137,787	100.0%
Variable Costs	(2,630,547)	51.2%
Cont. Margin	2,507,240	48.8%
Fixed Costs	(1,922,240)	
Depreciation Exp.	(125,000)	
E.B.I.T.	460,000	100.0%
Taxes	115,000	25.0%
NOPAT	345,000	75.0%
Capital Charge	(345,000)	
Residual Income	(0)	

"Is this good or bad?"

"You had total revenue of $5,000,000 as compared to a GBER of $5,137,787. This would mean that you are not covering all your operating costs, financing costs, and tax costs. You were in the black on your earnings and even NOPAT looked to be a pretty robust number, but in reality with a very aggressive growth expectation, you are not yet where you need to be. Let's recast the GBER format with your $5,000,000 revenue (Figure 9-14)."

Figure 9-14

---

[19] http://en.wikipedia.org/wiki/Residual_income_valuation

Global Break-Even Revenue

	Amount	%
Revenue	5,000,000	100.0%
Variable Costs	(2,560,000)	51.2%
Cont. Margin	2,440,000	48.8%
Fixed Costs	(1,922,240)	
Depreciation Exp.	(125,000)	
E.B.I.T.	392,760	100.0%
Taxes	98,190	25.0%
NOPAT	294,570	75.0%
Capital Charge	(345,000)	
Residual Income	(50,430)	

"Your residual income is a negative $50,430.

"I'm a little stunned," she admitted.

"A lot of companies are in the same boat. They just don't realize the full cost of equity and in particular the impact that growth has on Invested Capital needs. Now if you were above GBER then you would be adding value to the business, but as it is, you are consuming value."

"What do you mean adding or consuming value? My clients receive great value from me. My clothes and accessories are of the highest quality and the women who purchase them and wear them are richer for it."

"I don't question that, but as a company you are not worth what has been invested in it."

305

"I'm confused."

"Well, if I was going to buy your company, I wouldn't pay more than book value and perhaps not even that much."

"What is book value and what do you mean?"

"If I subtract the $500,000 loan from your Financing Capital, I end up with $750,000. That is the book value of your equity. If I was going to buy your business right now I'm not sure I would pay more than that to acquire your equity. Of course this gets into a whole other discussion."

Just then the attendant announced that the lights would be going down so people could sleep on this overnight flight.

Full Circle

When he awoke, he looked over to see her curled up, her head resting on a flight pillow and a flight blanket covering her body. The light was streaming through a couple of windows whose shades had been raised. The other passengers were in various stages of sleep and partial awareness. A few were wandering the aisles and stretching their legs.

He sensed it was time for another visit to the restroom so he got up and went to the door. The small sliding sign said "Occupied," so he leaned against the bulkhead waiting his turn.

When he had gained access and found the relief the lavatory provided he opened the door to see her standing there, waiting to be next to use the facility. He sized her up to be about five foot seven, several inches shorter than he was. "Good morning," he greeted her.

She nodded acknowledgment, let him pass, entered the facility, and closed the door. He returned to his seat just as the lights were activated, illuminating the whole area.

When she returned, he got up to let her into the aisle and then settled down again. She didn't appear to be a morning person and was quiet and withdrawn.

The attendant was upon him with pre-breakfast service. He washed his hands with the hot hand towel and curiously watched the others around him.

They sat in silence eating their breakfast as he explored the offerings on the TV screen imbedded in the back of the seat in front of him.

When the breakfast trays were taken away and as he nursed a cup of coffee, he heard, "How did you sleep?" He turned, and she seemed to have come back to life.

"Not very well," he said, "and you?"

"Surprisingly well," she responded.

He assumed their discussion of the previous night was concluded until she spoke up. "I was wondering how I could be doing so well and yet have a residual income, as you call it. What can I do to correct the problem?"

"There are a lot of ways to make the situation better. One way is to reduce your Invested Capital, another is to reduce your weighted average cost of capital, and yet another is to reduce your variable and fixed costs. You could also raise the prices of your goods and generate more revenue per item."

"I guess I could raise prices or cut expenses. I feel that I'm already well positioned and don't know what that would do. I will have to think about that," she mused. "By reducing my weighted average cost of capital you mean I would be lowering my expectations of what I was taking out of the business as a dividend?"

"That's right, but based on my experience with very small companies like yours the expectations of the owner/managers is usually higher than the one we calculated of 47.3%," he noted.

"What do I do then?" she asked.

"Let's get back to your working capital policies." He turned the pages back to their initial calculations. "You have 55 days in accounts receivable, 24 days in inventory, and 45 days in accounts payable. All of these numbers directly affect your Invested Capital. If you reduce your accounts receivable and inventory balances your Invested Capital will go down and your residual income goes up. Likewise, if you increase your accounts payable balance and extend your payment days to more than 45 this will also lower your Invested Capital."

"In today's economic climate I'm just afraid my accounts receivable credit may have to go even higher.

I've already pushed by suppliers about as hard as I can by paying them in 45 days. I'm fearful they may want quicker payment and those days will have to come down," she worried.

"If you lower your accounts payable or increase your accounts receivable then Invested Capital will go up and you will be in an ever worst Residual Income position."

"It is really interesting how it all ties together," she pondered. My sense is that you aren't simply teasing me here and really setting me up for an ongoing consulting engagement," she questioned.

"Remember our agreement---no names, no strings, and no follow-up. Let's just celebrate the moment and leave it at that," he responded. He decided to pull back a little now and not go into all the specifics of a more precise valuation for her. It appeared she could sense this and didn't press the issue. They both pulled away.

He unzipped his GBER-marked executive case and began pouring over the presentation he was about to give, while she reviewed more data from her business. Occasionally they offered a passing comment to each other, but he realized nothing would come from this and it was basically over.

The plane touched down and everyone anxiously waited for the outer door to open and spill passengers onto the jet way and into the terminal. Finally, the seatbelt light went off and everyone stood up. He focused on extracting his carryon from the overhead bin and working his way to the passageway.

As he walked along, he felt a slight tug on his shirt-sleeve and turning to see her walking beside him. She leaned toward him and said, "I will be having dinner alone tonight on the Bateaux Dinner Cruise that leaves the terminal directly across from the Eiffel Tower at 9 pm. I think it is a real shame to have to eat alone."

This caught him off guard and he slowed his walk to contemplate what she had said. As he did, she moved past him, glanced back, offered him a confident smile and was off, lost in the crowd.

Am I Seine?

He stood high up on the Eiffel Tower and looked down at the Seine. He could see the bridge and the boat dock next to it. He looked at his watch; it was 8:30 pm. He wondered what might be waiting for him at that boat dock. Was she jesting or not?

As he slowly approached the dock, he scanned the crowd waiting there. It was a beautiful evening. The water danced and reflected the lights of the boats and the street lamps. He glanced in the direction of the Champs-Elysees and the lights of the city.

He rounded the corner, still uncertain that she would be there and if she was, could he find her? Did he really want to find her?

"There you are," he heard. He turned and saw her standing about fifteen feet away. She was wearing a simple white sleeveless dress with a scooped neckline and a dark accent belt. As she moved toward him the white fabric flowed with the motion of her body.

"What am I doing?" he thought to himself.

She approached him, smiled and putting her left arm through his, she motioned with her right arm toward the waiting boat. They descended the stairs and he felt a soft breeze off the water. Again, the thought echoed in his mind, "What am I doing?"

They were directed toward the front of the boat and a prime table. From here they could see everything. "Did you present today?" she asked.

"No, it's tomorrow at 10:00 am."

"I'm not going to ask if you have been to Paris before or what you did today. I love it when you talk about my business. You get so excited, and as crazy as it sounds, I find it really compelling and revealing."

Thoughts quickly shot through his head. Sure, on the flight the whole conversation was about her. He knew she was going to be disappointed with a follow-up without the confinement and protection of the plane, but wait---what did he care. She meant nothing to him and she was sucking him into her intimidating power again. "Okay, you asked for it, we are going to talk ethics."

"What do you mean?"

"You know, right and wrong---stuff like that."

It appeared that this wasn't exactly what she had in mind. After a pause she concluded, "You are full of surprises."

He had seized the moment and taken her completely off guard. "I have a total portrait of you except for what your ethical and moral standards are."

The boat was moving and Paris was indeed the city of lights with illuminated buildings passing by on both sides. A waiter began the food service as the first bridge passed overhead.

He looked over to see young couples on the broad walkway along the Seine. Some were holding hands and some locked in an embrace. Here he was with one of the most beautiful women he had ever met and in one of the most romantic settings, and he was going to talk about ethics! He braced himself and committed to resist being seduced by the elements around him.

"I have a theory about ethics," he offered.

"Yes, and what is that?" she responded, raising one eyebrow.

"I call it Me, We, or Thee. Are our actions influenced more by our own personal will, by family, friends and fraternal associations, or by science, sage or scripture?"

"I've never heard such a thing."

"Let me pose a couple of moral dilemmas and you tell me how you would respond."

"Okay."

"What do you do with unwanted customers, people who come to your shop that you would rather not serve?"

She was taken aback. "You go right for the jugular. Here let me claw you away from my neck," She motioned as though to tear his hand from that beautiful pedestal on which her flawless head rested.

"Well, what do you do" he pressed.

"There are people who come to the shop that simply shouldn't be there. They are dressed inappropriately and would detract from the image we are trying to project, or they obviously don't have the resources and could occupy a great deal of our time without making the sale."

"So how do you deal with it?"

"We certainly don't ignore the problem but instead confront it head on. We efficiently assess the situation, greet the person, determine their needs and try to direct them to the appropriate place where there needs can best be fulfilled. We suggest, with great care and tact, that they might find exactly what they are looking for at the store across the street.

"How did you arrive at that solution? Did you initiate it from your own wisdom, did you adopt it from what you observed peers were doing, or is there some industry sage who you look to for advice on such issues?"

"I think it came from my previous employers where I learned how to run a store."

"Okay, next situation, how would you handle a rich celebrity who was caught taking things without paying for them?"

"You are cruel and go right to the heart of the matter," she said, putting her clasped hands to the middle of her chest, emphasizing her breasts.

He was trying to remain on a very high business level and an ethical one at that, and every action she offered drew him back to her sensuality.

She thought for a moment. "We had a situation like this and it was probably one of the most difficult things I've ever had to deal with. Even though we caught this woman red handed outside the store with items she had not paid for in her bag, it was still her word against ours."

"The first time we observed her on our hidden camera, the items were not very expensive and we wrote it off. The second time is when we caught her outside the store."

"Do you believe in grace or punishment? he asked.

"I would like to say grace with some latitude, but for chronic offenders, you have to initiate tough love. You love them, but you are tough. We let her know we were aware of her actions and promised to prosecute if it ever happened again."

"Where did that policy come from? Did you unilaterally come up with it, did it come from your prior experience, or is it based on some sage, scientific study or scriptural doctrine?"

"I think mostly from my previous employment, but it could be a merging of all of the above."

Just then they looked up to see another bridge pass overhead and the magnificent lights on the buildings around which were in turn reflected on the water.

The Final Question

"Let's go with one last question," he proposed.

"That sounds great," she concluded.

"Where do we go from here?"

She sat back in her chair and her eyes looked deep into his. "You know a great deal more about me that I do about you. Neither of us knows if the other is involved with someone or even married. We don't even know each other's names. I'm not sure."

He looked away at the water and could see the lights illuminating on the upcoming bridge.

She spoke up softly, "If someone were to try and find your lecture tomorrow, where would they go?"

He smiled.

Summary of Concepts

Accrual Accounting
Accrual accounting helps to smooth things out and reflects a matching of revenues earned and the expenses that generated those revenues.

Accounts Receivable
If I divide the $325,000 in accounts receivable by your sales per day, you have about 24 days of sales that are uncollected at any one time.

Extending Credit
She wanted to set up a revolving account and charge it. I saw this as a way to capture even more of her business and establish a permanent customer.

Inventory
Dividing the $300,000 inventory by the $5,500 in the cost of daily sales indicates that an item will remain on the racks for almost 55 days before it goes out the door.

Power Trio
The two operating assets we just discussed, accounts receivable and inventory, plus one of your operating liabilities, accounts payable, I refer to as the power trio.

Accounts Payable
If I divide your daily sales of $5,500 into the $250,000 of accounts payable, it tells me that from the time you receive your goods it takes you about 45 days to pay the vendors.

Financing versus Operating
The decision regarding how much to borrow, is completely independent from the ongoing operations of the business.

Interest Expense
If we didn't have the interest expense, then the income tax would be much higher. We say that interest expense provides a tax break.

Income Tax Rate
Taxes were $33,000, so if I add that back to the Net Income of $100,000, the before tax amount would be $133,000. It looks like the tax rate was about 25%, or $33,000 taxes on $133,000 of before-tax income.

Net Income versus NOPAT
Instead of $100,000 of Net Income, we now have $145,000 NOPAT or Net Operating Profit After-Taxes.

After-Tax cost of Debt
If I count that $15,000 in tax savings because of the interest expense, then the true cost is $45,000 divided by $500,000 or about 9%.

Hidden Dividends
That's $200,000 (for management and buying) compared to the $400,000 you are taking. The difference of $200,000 is really a dividend or a return on your equity investment as an owner.

Net Income versus NOPAT
That is true. If we look at the newly adjusted NOPAT of $295,000 we find three things there: $100,000 of original Net Income, $150,000 of net dividends to equity holders

and $45,000 of net interest expense. The first two belong to the equity investors, it's just that $100,000 is reinvested back into the company on the equity holder's behalf and the $150,000 is paid out as a dividend.

Invested Capital Structure Weights
Let's see---$500,000 of debt divided by $1,250,000 Invested Capital is 40% and $750,000 Equity divided by the same $1,250,000 is 60%.

Weighted Average Cost of Capital
If we multiply the weight of debt times the after-tax cost of debt we get a component cost of 3.6%. Then if we multiply the weight of equity times the cost of equity we get a component cost of 19.8%. Adding these two components together we get a weighted average cost of 23.4%.

Revenue versus Units
I have determined the easiest way to equate everything on a relative scale is to talk in terms of price and total revenue instead of total units.

Relevant Range
Over a short period which we call the relevant range, some of your costs will remain the same irrespective of the level of sales. Other costs will go up and down as revenue moves up or down. Over a short period of time we try to find how much will fit into either category.

Fixed and Variable Formula
The y is the operating expense level and the x is the revenue. As the revenue changes, it will dictate a specific expense level to match the sales. The 480.56 is the level of fixed costs. Regardless of the level of revenue there

will be $480,560 in expenses every quarter over a relevant range. So from this you know that every quarter you will have at least that much in costs and expenses.

Variable Costs
That is the variable cost piece. For every dollar in revenue you will incur 51.2 cents in costs.

Break-Even Formula
Most educational programs that teach Break-Even use a model where fixed costs are divided by the contribution margin percentage to arrive at the required revenue.

Contribution Margin Percent
The contribution margin is the reciprocal of the variable cost number. For every dollar of revenue you have 51.2 cents or 51.2 percent in variable costs. All the rest of the excess revenue contributes to paying for the fixed costs. In your case it would be $1.00 minus .512 or .488 cents. This can also be stated in percentage terms as 48.8% of revenue goes to covering fixed costs.

Capital Charge
So, a WACC of 23.4% times total Invested Capital of $1,250,000 is $292,500. I call this my capital charge.

CPSIA information can be obtained at www.ICGtesting.com
Printed in the USA
LVOW13s2200200214

374622LV00001B/61/P